A Saved People

Lee Roy Martin

Cover photo from Storm/stock.adobe.com.

ISBN: 978-1-940682-56-3

Printed in the United States of America.

TABLE OF CONTENTS

ACKNOWLEDGMENTS

I would like to offer my thanks to Dr. O. Wayne and Rev. Pamela R. Brewer, serving as Directors of Men's Discipleship and Women's Discipleship, respectively, for their invitation to contribute to the Living What We Believe discipleship series. Wayne and Pamela believe very strongly in the power of the Word of God to change lives.

The origin and shape of this project owes much also to Rev. Ben Wiles. The Lord has given Ben a burden to teach pastors and lay people the important aspects of our faith. He insists that if our faith is genuine, then it must be lived out every day.

I appreciate my wife Karen (a retired high school English teacher) for reading and correcting my manuscript with her customary enthusiasm and encouragement. I also appreciate the editorial work of Lenae S. Simmons, who serves as the Executive Secretary for Church of God Adult Discipleship.

The content of this volume owes much to the following works of scholarship:

Daniel L. Akin, David P. Nelson, and Peter R. Schemm, *A Theology for the Church* (Nashville, TN: B & H Academic, 2007).

French L. Arrington, *Exploring the Declaration of Faith* (Cleveland, TN: Pathway Press, 2003).

Kenneth J. Collins, *The Theology of John Wesley: Holy Love and the Shape of Grace* (Nashville, TN: Abingdon Press, 2007).

R. Hollis Gause, *Living in the Spirit: The Way of Salvation* (Cleveland, TN: CPT Press, Rev. and expanded edn, 2009).

—Lee Roy Martin

FOREWORD

Why Living What We Believe?

Why indeed? The Living What We Believe six-volume series of small group/class studies is written and specifically developed for the purpose of making Pentecostal disciples of Jesus Christ. For those seeking to know more about living the Christ-life, there is plenty here to be learned and discussed. However, Living What We Believe (all six volumes) has much more to offer than biblical knowledge and doctrine alone. This series has been especially created to foster relational discipleship within a community of believers for the purpose of transformational life-change! Making disciples is all about developing true followers of Jesus Christ while understanding that the person and work of the Holy Spirit himself is intimately and undeniably involved in this lifelong process. It is the Holy Spirit who helps disciples become more like Jesus.

The Living What We Believe six-volume series is a complete 24-week discipleship study (though a participant or group is free to use any one volume alone, or in any order they prefer). This series both understands and is built upon the truth that only disciples make other disciples! Coming together as the body of Christ within the context of a small group is an essential and fruitful means by which Jesus' Great Commission (Matthew 28:18-20), can be fulfilled. Likewise, coming together as the body of Christ within the context of a small group is also a natural and organic means by which Jesus' Great Commandment (Matthew 22:36-40) can find a more productive fulfillment.

Over the course of the six volumes of this series, the reader/participant will be provided both biblical/ doctrinal teaching based on the fourteen points of the Church of God Declaration of Faith as well as the opportunity to reflect upon and discuss the practical ramifications of living out what we believe . . . all within the relational context of small group discipleship. The general framework of the series is based upon, and generally guided by an understanding of the "Fivefold Gospel" (i.e. Jesus is our Savior, Jesus is our Sanctifier, Jesus is our Spirit-Baptizer, Jesus is our Healer, and Jesus is our coming King).

The format of the Living What We Believe series is simple, relational and structured specifically to make true disciples, as well as assisting disciple-makers to fulfill their mission. Each of the six volumes, (*A Believing People, A Saved People, A Sanctified People, A Spirit-Baptized People, A Healed People, An Expectant People*) is a four-week study with each week divided into five days. Each participant reads, reflects, and reacts to each of these days at home in his or her personal time. Each day will feature several components which enable the growth process of the disciple at a personal level:

- Search the Scripture (selected Scripture readings).
- Answer the Following Questions (reflective questions directly relevant to the Scripture selection).
- Yield to the Spirit—divided into three sub-sections:
    1. "Know"—relating to one's intellect.
    2. "Be"—relating to one's passion (their heart).
    3. "Do"—relating to one's behavior (their hands).
- Offer a Prayer—the conclusion of each day.

After the five daily personal interactions, the participant will join with the other members (who have likewise personally worked through the sessions) for the weekly small group session. Led by the leader/facilitator, the weekly small group meetings provide members with the time to open up, give responses, and yield to the corporate and personal leading of the Holy Spirit. The leader/facilitator does not decide the response from members, but rather asks questions and helps guide group members to the practical, behavioral outworking of what we believe as Pentecostal members of the body of Christ. Each group session is about sharing, relating, learning, and being aware of the presence of the Holy Spirit. There will be a key scripture for discussion in each group session. As you work through the studies, you will note information about the "Opening," "Prayer," "Testimony," "Discussion Questions," and the section we refer to as "Yielding to the Spirit." Group leaders will find much more very helpful information concerning both starting and leading a small group from series Assistant Editor J. Ben Wiles in the following sections of this volume. If you are a group leader/facilitator, always make sure to publicly welcome the presence of the Holy Spirit to guide, teach, convict, encourage, and unify all those who are present for the weekly group session. Remember that the ultimate benefit of the Living What We Believe discipleship series is not only the transmission of biblical/doctrinal teaching, but also it is the Spirit-led, life-transformation of men and women into healthy disciples of Jesus Christ!

As general editor and publishers of this disciple-making series, we wish to express our thanks and sincere appreciation to Assistant Editor J. Ben Wiles, whose *People of the Spirit* served as the primary template for Living What We Believe. We also wish to thank Lenae Simmons for her diligent labor in the copy editing, layout, and design of this work. Finally, we wish to convey our respect and gratitude to the scholars who authored the individual volumes:

Volume One—*A Believing People* by J. Ben Wiles

Volume Two—*A Saved People* by Lee Roy Martin

Volume Three—*A Sanctified People* by J. Ben Wiles

Volume Four—*A Spirit-Baptized People* by French L. Arrington

Volume Five—*A Healed People* by Daniel Tomberlin

Volume Six—*An Expectant People* by French L. Arrington

These authors and their insightful work and commitment to making disciples for Jesus Christ cannot be overstated.

Whether Pentecostal, evangelical, or any believer wishing to take up the cross and follow Jesus, we highly recommend all six volumes of the Living What We Believe series. If you are a disciple-maker, this series is at your service. While it can certainly be used for individual study, we highly recommend this small group experience.

O. Wayne Brewer, D.Min
Men's Discipleship

Pamela R. Brewer, M.A.
Women's Discipleship

Adult Discipleship Church of God International Offices

General Editors: O. Wayne and Pamela R. Brewer
Assistant Editor: J. Ben Wiles
Chief Copy Editor, Layout, and Design: Lenae Simmons

PREFACE

How to Start a Living What We Believe Group

The following steps are important in the process of starting a group in your local church:

1. Pray and seek the leadership of the Holy Spirit to make sure He is calling you to lead a Living What We Believe group.

2. Secure permission from the pastor of your local church to lead the group.

3. Find an appropriate location that is conducive to the group encounters—either in the church facility or in a host home. Public areas such as coffee shops are not appropriate, as they would potentially hinder the group's ability to fully engage the leading of the Spirit during times of prayer.

4. Set a time and place for the first meeting.

5. Develop the group through invitation. Your goal is clear: to lead every member of the group to grow in Jesus Christ, and to discover and fulfill God's personal call on his or her life in the power

of the Holy Spirit. This is a transformation group where every member will grow and be fully involved in the discipleship process personally and by leading others in the discipleship process. Select four or, at most, five people to be in your group. Include at least one mature believer and at least one new believer. (Note: a group with four to five people is best for a study such as this one. However, if you need to have a larger group, you should not have more than 10 to 12 people).

6. Decide how you are going to handle childcare.
7. Determine the cost for the group. Group members should purchase their own copy of the student guides for each unit, unless the church has opted to make other arrangements.
8. Order materials in plenty of time to have them for the first group encounter.
9. Read through the leader's guide and acclimate yourself to the Living What We Believe discipleship process.

Keys to Successfully Leading a Small Group

1. Get to know the group members.

2. Encourage participation by everyone. Remember that discipleship and lecturing are not the same thing. You are a facilitator, and your job is to facilitate participation that leads to transformation for everyone!

    - Communicate your expectation that everyone participates.
    - Ask questions.
    - Make it fulfilling so they want to return.
    - Reduce and eliminate embarrassing and threatening situations.
    - Protect and honor confidentiality within the group.

3. Affirming vs. Endorsing

    - It is important that, as the leader, you affirm all the responses. You say, "Thank you, Ben," or "That's very interesting, Elizabeth." No matter what the participants say, don't criticize their remarks. What they just said may be antagonistic to you or it may simply sound ridiculous, but don't directly criticize it. Instead, say something like, "Well, that's interesting. What do the rest of you think?" Once you, as the leader, directly disapprove of someone's comments, then some people will never speak up again. They're going to fear disapproval; once exploration stops for them, the journey does too. On the other side of the coin, while it's important to affirm all responses, avoid the temptation to endorse them. Don't say things like, "Now that's a great comment," or "I couldn't agree with you more." Such endorsements tip your hand and leave others feeling like their comments are not acceptable. Also, resist the urge to be too instructional, trying to answer everyone's questions and solve everyone's problems. Once a know-it-all person speaks up, conversation tends to shut down. You can give your own opinion, but do it in a personal and humble way. Maybe you could say, "My experience has been . . ." or "This is how I see it . . ."

4. Remember the four C's of the facilitator's role:
   - **Content**—Keep the group grounded in Scripture.

- **Care**—Be sensitive to the feelings, needs, and life situations of the group members.
- **Commitment**—Demonstrate your commitment to completing the Living What We Believe process completely and thoroughly. Model your commitment by your careful preparation as the facilitator for each of the group encounters.
- **Consistency**—Follow up consistently with established schedules and routines for the group. Your consistent approach to the process will inspire the same in the participants. Also, a consistently positive attitude will go a long way to establishing a healthy environment for the group to flourish.

5. Manage difficult and challenging personalities in your group so they don't hijack the encounters.
   - The Talking Hijacker answers every question before anyone else can respond. In her book, *Help! My Small Group Has Been Hijacked!, Four Common Hijackers and ways to Respond*, Margaret Feinberg discusses helpful responses to potential small group "Hijackings."
     - Your first course of action is to pull them aside in a one-on-one meeting. Thank

them for their participation, but be honest with them about the need for others to participate. Consider some practical ways you could offer to help them do that (respond only to every second or third question, keep responses short, and so forth).

- Your second course of action (if the first course of action doesn't work) is to change the discussion time to a more structured format. For example, you call on people for answers.

- The Emotional Hijacker shows up every week with an emotional crisis.
  - The first course of action is to spend some one-on-one time with this person and allow him or her to emotionally unpack with you. If necessary, recommend a good counselor or a conversation with the pastor. This may alleviate the problem in the group encounter.
  - If the first course of action doesn't resolve the issue, you may need to remind the group of the task at hand, which is to work through the material, and that extra questions can be raised at the end of the session.

- **Note**: there may be a person in your group who is just going through a difficult time and is not truly an emotional hijacker. Be open to the leading of the Holy Spirit to allow a short time of personal ministry to this person if you feel it is appropriate; then return to the material at hand for that group encounter.

6. The Leader Hijacker is a backseat driver who is constantly making suggestions about how you should lead the group.
   - The first course of action is to have a one-on-one conversation with the individual. Sift through his or her comments to see if you can glean anything helpful. Sometimes, there will be good suggestions that can benefit the group. If so, mention these helpful suggestions in your conversation, which will keep the atmosphere positive. Politely ask the leader hijacker to stop doing so at the group encounters by pointing out that he/she can lead to disunity in the group.

   - If the hijacker does it in another meeting, simply say, "We can talk about suggestions outside of the group encounter," then continue with the material at hand.

7. The Late Hijacker constantly walks into the group encounter late, disrupting the group and causing a loss of momentum and focus.

    - Discuss the situation directly with the individual and encourage him or her to make every effort to arrive on time. If that is not possible, encourage him or her to arrive quietly and discreetly so as to not disturb the group. They should also consider waiting outside if it seems to be a particularly sensitive moment.

    - If the individual continues to disrupt the group, consider privately encouraging them to find another group to join that would work better with his or her schedule.

8. Remember, you are accountable for your stewardship of the group!

    - Care for them enough that you refuse to accept poor decisions or justification for inconsistent participation.

    - Don't be judgmental. Address behaviors only—don't try to guess the motivation behind them.

    - Pray regularly over the group.

- See yourself as a mentor/role model.
- Encourage authentic relationships and conversations in the group by modeling them. Be yourself and be real, but also be holy and be humble!
- Trust God. Whatever is accomplished is by Him and through Him and for His glory. It is His will for you and your group to succeed and He is ready to give you the grace to do so!

Group Covenant

> Instead, speaking the truth in love, we will grow to become in every respect the mature body of him who is the head, that is, Christ. From him the whole body, joined and held together by every supporting ligament, grows and builds itself up in love, as each part does its work (Ephesians 4:15-16 NIV).

It is hoped that each individual undertaking the Living What We Believe process will experience transformation and growth in Christlikeness over the course of the experience. But individual growth alone is not enough. It must take place in the context of relationship with others of the same faith, each one building the others up so that all become mature followers of Jesus Christ and, as a result, fully functioning participants in God's plan to save creation. With that in mind, before continuing with the study, each member of the group should agree to the following covenant with one another. Please read and reflect upon the following statements and indicate your commitment to the group by signing your name at the bottom. Then each member of the Living What We Believe group should sign one another's group covenant so that everyone's copy has every signature of the group. Keep this group covenant in your book for future reference as needed.

GROUP COVENANT

PRIORITY: The group meeting will be a priority in my schedule. If I am running late or unable to attend, I will contact my group leader.

PREPAREDNESS: I realize that what I put into the lesson is what I will get out of it. Therefore, I will prepare for the lesson each week and come prepared to share.

RESPECT: Everyone has a right to his or her opinion and all questions are encouraged and respected. I will listen attentively to others without interrupting them.

CONFIDENTIALITY: Anything of a personal nature that is said in the meeting should not be repeated outside the meeting. This group is intended to be a safe place for open discussion and sharing.

HONESTY: I will strive to be real, honest, and transparent with the other group members.

SUPPORT: The mission and values of the group have my support, and I will refrain from gossip or criticism.

SIGNATURES DATE

A SAVED PEOPLE

Introduction

We are a saved people. We were lost, but now we are found. We were blind, but now we can see. We were sinners, but now we are the children of God. We walked in darkness, but now we walk in the light. We have been saved by grace. We have been saved by the precious blood of Jesus.

As a saved people, we are a joyful people. After the Lord saved Israel from Egyptian bondage, Moses declared to them, "Happy are you, O Israel! Who is like you, a people saved by the LORD?" (Deuteronomy 33:29). As a saved people, we are also an active people. We were saved by grace, and we were "created in Christ Jesus for good works" (Ephesians 2:10).

The day that you became a Christian, you experienced both a conclusion and a beginning. You were dead in your sins, but Christ made you alive in Him (Colossians 2:13). The moment that Christ entered your heart, your old life was over, and a new life began. You became a "new creature; old things have passed away; behold all things have become new" (2 Corinthians 5:17).

Therefore, entrance into new life is symbolized by the term "born again" (John 3:3-7). For example, the birth of a child is a beginning, not an ending. The baby embarks on the journey of a lifetime, a journey of learning and relating to other people. Similarly, when we are born again, we embark on our Christian journey. Perhaps you became a Christian many years ago; or you may have been saved only recently. Either way, you are on a journey with God and with fellow believers. You are seeking a city, "whose builder and maker is God" (Hebrews 11:10).

The purpose of this study is to guide you on your journey with God as you live out your "salvation with fear and trembling" (Philippians 2:12). The fact that the way of salvation is a journey is emphasized in the Bible by the use of the term "way" and "walk." Our "walk" is our behavior, our habits, and our character. A "way" is a pathway, a certain pattern and direction of life. There are essentially two ways: the "way" that leads to life and the "way" that leads to death. The Lord commanded Abraham, "walk before Me and be blameless" (Genesis 17:1). Israel was instructed "to walk in" God's ways (Deuteronomy 8:6) and to "walk in the light of the LORD" (Isaiah 2:5). Jesus Christ opened for us "a new and living way" (Hebrews 10:20). As believers, we are told to "walk honestly" (Romans 13:13 KJV), to "walk by faith, not by sight" (2 Corinthians 5:7), to "walk in the Spirit" (Galatians 5:25), and to "walk in love, as Christ also has loved us and given Himself for us" (Ephesians 5:2).

This study is an invitation for you to renew your walk with God. To strengthen you in your walk, this book series unfolds and explains the daily relevance of the Church of God Declaration of Faith. The entire Declaration of Faith is as follows:

We Believe:

1. In the verbal inspiration of the Bible.
2. In one God eternally existing in three persons; namely, the Father, Son, and Holy Ghost.
3. That Jesus Christ is the only begotten Son of the Father, conceived of the Holy Ghost, and born of the Virgin Mary. That Jesus was crucified, buried, and raised from the dead. That He ascended to heaven and is today at the right hand of the Father as the Intercessor.
4. That all have sinned and come short of the glory of God and that repentance is commanded of God for all and necessary for forgiveness of sins.
5. That justification, regeneration, and the new birth are wrought by faith in the blood of Jesus Christ.
6. In sanctification subsequent to the new birth, through faith in the blood of Christ; through the Word, and by the Holy Ghost.
7. Holiness to be God's standard of living for His people.

8. In the baptism with the Holy Ghost subsequent to a clean heart.
9. In speaking with other tongues as the Spirit gives utterance and that it is the initial evidence of the baptism of the Holy Ghost.
10. In water baptism by immersion, and all who repent should be baptized in the name of the Father, and of the Son, and of the Holy Ghost.
11. Divine healing is provided for all in the atonement.
12. In the Lord's Supper and washing of the saints' feet.
13. In the premillennial second coming of Jesus. First, to resurrect the righteous dead and to catch away the living saints to Him in the air. Second, to reign on the earth a thousand years.
14. In the bodily resurrection; eternal life for the righteous, and eternal punishment for the wicked.

For the next four weeks, we will be looking at statements four and five, and we will use them as our entry point to reading Scripture. These statements of our faith are:

> **"We believe that all have sinned and come short of the glory of God and that repentance is commanded of God for all and necessary for forgiveness of sins."**
>
> **"We believe that justification, regeneration, and the new birth are wrought by faith in the blood of Jesus Christ."**

These two statements of faith describe our experience of conversion. They tell us that everyone needs the Savior. Without Christ, everyone is separated from God and is powerless to save themselves. However, we read in the New Testament that "God so loved the world that He gave His only begotten Son, that whosoever believes in Him should not perish but have everlasting life" (John 3:16). Jesus willingly laid down His life and suffered on the cross so that every sinner could be saved. If we are to receive the free gift of salvation, we must believe on the Lord and repent of our sins.

As soon as we repent, God grants to us "justification," which means that He forgives our sins and declares us to be righteous. At the same time, the Holy Spirit enters our hearts and does the work of "regeneration, and the new birth," which means simply that we are made a new creation. We are born again. We who were dead are alive in Jesus Christ! Praise God! This powerful work of God is accomplished in us "through faith in the blood of Jesus Christ." We are not saved by our works, but by faith in Christ. The apostle Paul writes, "not by works of righteousness which we have done, but according to His mercy He saved us, through the washing of regeneration and renewing of the Holy Spirit" (Titus 3:5).

If we will open up ourselves to the Holy Spirit as we study together, God will encourage us, strengthen us, and guide us into a deeper walk with Him. Learning what it means to live a repentant lifestyle and to trust in God for our righteousness will give us assurance and make us more devoted to Christ.

As we walk with God, the world will see our good works and glorify the Father in heaven (Matthew 5:16). By living our faith and walking out our salvation, we will be a light and a witness to the world. We will be an example to our families, and we will be a blessing to other believers. If we are a saved people, then let us live out our salvation to the glory of God.

DECLARATION OF FAITH

◆◆◆◆◆◆◆◆

"We Believe . . .

That all have sinned and come short of the glory of God and that repentance is commanded of God for all and necessary for forgiveness of sins."

Week 1

BROKEN RELATIONSHIP

Week 1

Day 1

The Way Back to God

DECLARATION OF FAITH

"We Believe . . .

That all have sinned and come short of the glory of God and that repentance is commanded of God for all and necessary for forgiveness of sins."

Words to Hide in Your Heart

As it is written: "There is none righteous, no, not one; there is none who understands; there is none who seeks after God. They have all turned aside; they have together become unprofitable; there is none who does good, no, not one" (Romans 3:10-12).

Touching Base

Salvation has both a divine dimension and a human dimension. On the divine side, God sent His Son into the world to die on the cross for all humanity. Because of Jesus' sacrificial life and death, God graciously forgives our sins. On the human side, it is our sinfulness that ruined our relationship with God and created the need for salvation in the first place. Everyone has sinned, and everyone is separated from God. Furthermore, it is our responsibility to repent when the Holy Spirit convicts us of our sins.

Our focus for the next two weeks will be on the human side of salvation. We will study the sinfulness of humanity and the necessity of repentance. This week, we will study the damaging effect of sin. Before we can understand how the doctrine of sin applies to our lives as people of the Spirit, we must first understand what it means! Our belief about the sinfulness of humanity comes directly from the following Scripture: "…for all have sinned and fall short of the glory of God" (Romans 3:23).

In the first three chapters of the Book of Romans, the apostle Paul explains that humanity is separated from God. The relationship between God and humanity is broken. We are powerless to restore the relationship—

only God can do it. Therefore, while we were still sinners, "Christ died for us" (Romans 5:8).

When Paul states that "all" have sinned, he is not exaggerating. There is no difference between people who were brought up in church and people who have never entered a church—all have sinned. It makes no difference if our parents were Christians or if they were unbelievers. We all have sinned.

The Bible describes sin in a number of ways; but essentially, sin is any action, attitude, or thought that falls short of the glory of God. The "glory of God" refers to the image of God that every human should reflect. Adam and Eve were created in God's image as a reflection of God's glory and honor. They were perfect in heart, mind, and will. They lived day-by-day for God and in communion with God. Their imitation of God meant that their lives reflected the glory of God. However, when they disobeyed God's command, they no longer embodied God's perfection. They became sinners, living in rebellion against God. Their personal relationship with God was broken by their unbelief and pride.

Searching the Scripture

Read 1 John 1:8-10

> If we say that we have no sin, we deceive ourselves, and the truth is not in us. If we confess our sins, He is faithful and just to forgive us our sins and to cleanse us from all unrighteousness. If we say that we have not sinned, we make Him a liar, and His word is not in us.

Read Psalm 51:1-4:

> Have mercy upon me, O God, according to Your lovingkindness; according to the multitude of Your tender mercies, blot out my transgressions. Wash me thoroughly from my iniquity, and cleanse me from my sin. For I acknowledge my transgressions, and my sin is always before me. Against You, You only, have I sinned, and done this evil in Your sight—that You may be found just when You speak, and blameless when You judge.

Answer the Following Questions:

1. According to 1 John, whom do we deceive if we say that we have no sin? Whom do we make a liar? What is not in us?

2. Psalm 51 gives four different words for David's immoral acts: transgression, iniquity, sin, evil. Look up these words in the dictionary, and explain the difference between them.

3. Why do you suppose that David says to God, "Against You, You only, have I sinned"? Did he not sin against Bathsheba and Uriah?

Yielding to the Spirit

—Know—

It is important that we understand the universal sinfulness of humanity. The first step in receiving salvation is the knowledge that we have offended God and that we are separated from God because of our sins. Furthermore, when we share our faith with others, we must not mistakenly think that some people are "OK" without Christ. It is true that some people have better morals than other people, but our best is not sufficient to gain eternal life. We all need Jesus Christ.

—Be—

When the apostle Paul spoke about his sin, he did so with humility and with gratitude for God's forgiveness. He wrote the following testimony to Timothy:

> Christ Jesus came into the world to save sinners, of whom I am chief. However, for this reason I obtained mercy, that in me first Jesus Christ might show all longsuffering, as a pattern to those who are going to believe on Him for everlasting life (1 Timothy 1:15-16).

Like Paul, our admission of guilt should cause us to be humble. Without Christ, we are eternally lost. Also, the recognition of our sin should be the occasion for rejoicing that God has saved us. We were sinners, but God has forgiven our sins. Our relationship to God has been restored, and we walk with God daily.

—Do—

Although we were born into sin, we are no longer sinners. If we are born of God, we have eternal life in us and we can resist temptation. However, consider the following advice from 1 John 2:1:

> My little children, these things I write to you, so that you may not sin. And if anyone sins, we have an Advocate with the Father, Jesus Christ the righteous.

God's grace is sufficient to keep us from sinning; but if we sin, we can confess our sins and Jesus Christ will be our advocate with the Father. If you realize that you have committed a sin, confess it immediately and ask for God's forgiveness. Genuine confession will bring restoration.

Offer a Prayer

Lord, I admit that my sins have separated me from You. Like everyone else, I have fallen short of the glory for which You created me. But now I rejoice in Your salvation. I give thanks for Your mercy and abounding love. Give me the ability and the courage to share Your love with others who need You. In Jesus' name, I pray. Amen.

Day 2

In the Beginning

Searching the Scripture

Read Genesis 1:26-28

> Then God said, "Let Us make man in Our image, according to Our likeness; let them have dominion over the fish of the sea, over the birds of the air, and over the cattle, over all the earth and over every creeping thing that creeps on the earth." So God created man in His own image; in the image of God He created him; male and female He created them. Then God blessed them, and God said to them, "Be fruitful and multiply; fill the earth and subdue it; have dominion over the fish of the sea, over the birds of the air, and over every living thing that moves on the earth."

Answer the Following Questions:

1. Which of God's creations are made in the image of God? man

2. Are both male and female made in the image of God? yes

3. How would you define the "image" and "likeness" of God as it relates to Adam and Eve?

Yielding to the Spirit

—Know—

Adam and Eve were our first human parents. They were created to have fellowship with God, to work in the Garden, and to rule over the earth as God's representatives. They were created without sin and without an inner tendency toward sin. They lived in a perfect environment and in perfect communion with God and with each other. Their minds, their wills, and their desires were in proper relation to God; therefore, they enjoyed the blessings of serenity and innocence.

To be created in the image of God includes three interrelated components: (1) the spiritual image; (2) the administrative image; and (3) the moral image.

The **spiritual image** means that Adam and Eve had a spiritual nature and an immortal soul. This spiritual nature gave them understanding, will, and liberty. Understanding is the power to distinguish truth from falsehood. The will has reference to the desires, inclinations, longings that were holy and righteous. The endowment of liberty is perhaps the most important of all. God created Adam and Eve as genuine partners in covenant. Their relationship to God and their worship of God were entirely voluntary. They were created to find their perfection and purpose in the holy love of God, a love that can only arise and thrive in freedom. Unfortunately, their liberty made them the serpent's object of temptation. Adam and Eve were created with the liberty to obey God or to disobey God.

The **administrative image** means that human beings are related not simply to one another and to God, but also to nature itself and other creatures. Adam and Eve were given dominion over every living thing on the earth. This dominion implies responsibility to serve as the dispenser of God's blessings to the rest of creation.

The **moral image** is the capacity to embody the righteousness of God and the love of God. The apostle Paul refers to the "image" of God as being "righteousness and true holiness" (Ephesians 4:24 and Colossians 3:10). The moral image sets humans apart from the rest of creation. Humans are the only earthly creatures who are able to know God, to worship God, and to love God. The moral image is also what makes sin possible. The moral image reflects the relationship between God and humans, but that relationship is perverted and distorted through the effects of sin.

—Be—

How does this truth transform us? The moral image of God is connected to God's moral law, which is the expression of God's loving and holy nature. When someone makes an excuse for sin, they might say, "I am only human," implying that to be human is equal to being sinful. However, humans were not created with a sinful nature. Adam and Eve were created in the perfect moral image of God.

In the beginning, there was no sin in the world. After God created Adam and Eve, He declared that everything was just as it should be. "God saw everything that He had made, and, behold, it was very good" (Genesis 1:31). God made humanity to be good, not evil. Although *fallen* human nature is corrupted by sin, original human nature was good; and, through Christ, it can be good again.

—Do—

John Wesley declared that love is the greatest expression of the image of God. Love is the brightness of God's glory. As we surrender our lives to God, we become more like Him. The image of God is renewed as we take upon ourselves the righteousness, holiness, and love of God.

Offer a Prayer

Lord God, I look to You as my creator. I thank You that I was created in Your image. Although I have sinned against You in the past, I pray that You will transform me by Your grace and create in me a new heart of love and obedience. Let the image of God be seen in me, in righteousness and in true holiness. I ask these things in the name of Jesus, our Lord and Savior. Amen.

Day 3

Hiding From God

Searching the Scripture

Read Genesis 3:1-10

> Now the serpent was more cunning than any beast of the field which the LORD God had made. And he said to the woman, "Has God indeed said, 'You shall not eat of every tree of the garden'?" And the woman said to the serpent, "We may eat the fruit of the trees of the garden; but of the fruit of the tree which is in the midst of the garden, God has said, 'You shall not eat it, nor shall you touch it, lest you die.'" Then the serpent said to the woman, "You will not surely die. For God knows that in the day you eat of it your eyes will be opened, and you will be like God, knowing good and evil."
>
> So when the woman saw that the tree was good for food, that it was pleasant to the eyes, and a tree desirable to make one wise, she took of its fruit and ate. She also gave to her husband with her, and he ate. Then the eyes of both of them were opened, and they knew that they were naked; and they sewed fig leaves together and made themselves coverings.
>
> And they heard the sound of the LORD God walking in the garden in the cool of the day, and Adam and his wife hid themselves from the presence of the LORD God among the trees of the garden. Then the LORD God called

to Adam and said to him, "Where are you?" So he said, "I heard Your voice in the garden, and I was afraid because I was naked; and I hid myself."

Answer the Following Questions:

1. Who initiated the temptation of Eve?

   Serpent

2. Why did Eve believe the Serpent rather than God?

   liked what she saw

3. Where was Adam? Why did he not intervene?

   He fell also

4. Why did Adam and Eve hide from God?

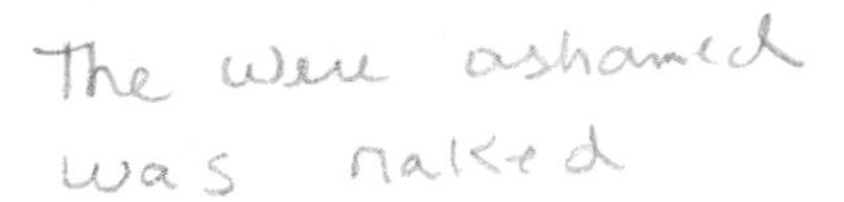

Yielding to the Spirit

—Know—

Adam and Eve were created in righteousness and holiness. They had no sin within themselves, but they were tempted from the outside, by the serpent. According to John Wesley, the root sin of Adam and Eve was **unbelief**. The serpent planted in Eve a seed of doubt when he asked, "Has God indeed said…?" As Eve looked upon the forbidden fruit, she began to doubt the word of God; and her doubt gave rise to pride; and her pride created self-will. Thus, her trusting relationship to God was broken. The apostle Paul states that Eve was deceived when she believed the lie of the serpent. Unbelief as the root of sin seems to be supported by Hebrews 3:12, which reads, "Beware, brethren, lest there be in any of you an evil heart of unbelief in departing from the living God."

Although the sin of pride caused the fall of Lucifer (Isaiah 14:12-14), the sin of Eve was not pride but unbelief. It was the perversion of the trusting relationship between God and humanity. Lack of trust in God always leads to alienation from God. Once alienated from God, every other sin comes easily.

The sin of Adam and Eve had tragic results. Adam had been warned, "of the tree of the knowledge of good and evil you shall not eat, for in the day that you eat of it you shall surely die" (Genesis 2:17). When they ate from the tree, they experienced both **physical** and **spiritual** effects. The sentence of death was passed on to their bodies. No longer would they walk in the life-sustaining presence of their creator. Adam brought pain, labor, and sorrow upon himself and all of his posterity.

Sin also resulted in horrible spiritual consequences. Along with physical death came spiritual and eternal death. The soul of Adam was separated from God. No longer did Adam enjoy the favor of God and intimate communion with God. His soul was dead to God.

Along with the loss of God's favor came the loss of the image of God. Adam's disobedience brought sin into the world and robbed humanity of God's image. Virtue, righteousness, and true holiness were gone, and humanity fell toward the image of the beasts, dominated by self-will and unholy passions.

The **spiritual image** of God in Adam was damaged but not completely destroyed by the Fall. Human understanding was now confused and often in error, mistaking falsehood for truth and truth for falsehood. The will of Adam was also corrupted, being dominated by evil desires such as anger, hatred, fear, and shame. When he sinned, Adam lost his liberty; for "whoever commits sin is a slave of sin" (John 8:34).

The **administrative image** of God in Adam was also damaged. Instead of being the conduit of blessings and grace to all creation, humanity became the abuser and destroyer of creation, selfishly consuming resources.

The **moral image** of God in Adam was greatly marred. No longer did Adam reflect the righteousness and holiness of his creator. The life of God was extinguished in the soul, and the glory departed from him. He was unholy; he was unhappy; he was full of sin, full of guilt, and tormented by fear.

—Be—

How does this truth transform us? How does it affect our daily lives? Since the Fall, no one has been able to escape their own sinfulness. Humanity may become more enlightened and more educated, but we are still tormented by hatred, lust, anger, and covetousness. We must take sin seriously, and we must take seriously the damage caused by sin.

We live in a world that is ravaged by the effects of Adam's sin. The apostle Paul states, "Therefore, just as through one man sin entered the world, and death through sin, and thus death spread to all men …" (Romans 5:12). Sickness, disease, suffering, and death are all around us. How shall we respond? We must confess that without Christ we all are lost. We must thank God that He offers a way of salvation. We must allow God to transform us by His grace and restore in us the beautiful and holy image of God. Paul declares that we are "being transformed into the same image from glory to glory, just as by the Spirit of the Lord" (2 Corinthians 3:18).

—Do—

Take a moment to prayerfully think about how the Lord has spoken to you through today's study. Have you considered the seriousness of disobedience to God? Do you value your personal relationship to God? Briefly describe your experience in two or three sentences on this page.

Offer a Prayer

Heavenly Father, I thank You for creating me in Your image and likeness. I thank You for giving me the liberty to know You, to serve You, to worship You, and to love You. I surrender my life to You today. I pray that You will transform me into the image and likeness of Jesus Christ. Open my eyes to see You, and open my ears to hear Your Word. As David prayed, "Search me, O God, and know my heart; Try me and know my thoughts and see if there be any wicked way in me, and lead me in the way everlasting." In Jesus' name. Amen.

Day 4

The Bondage of Sin

Searching the Scripture

Read Romans 3:9-18

> What then? Are we better than they? Not at all. For we have previously charged both Jews and Greeks that they are all under sin. As it is written: "There is none righteous, no, not one; There is none who understands; There is none who seeks after God. They have all turned aside; They have together become unprofitable; There is none who does good, no, not one." "Their throat is an open tomb; With their tongues they have practiced deceit"; "The poison of asps is under their lips"; "Whose mouth is full of cursing and bitterness." "Their feet are swift to shed blood; Destruction and misery are in their ways; And the way of peace they have not known." "There is no fear of God before their eyes."

Answer the Following Questions:

1. According to Paul, are all unbelievers equally guilty of sin? yes

2. Explain the three areas of human failure: (1) none righteous, (2) none who understands, and (3) none who seek after God.

1- ~~Yes~~ no one does good
2. Full of cursing
3. no fear

3. What do you think Paul means by the phrase, "They have together become unprofitable"?

Un Holy

4. Note the three references to aspects of the mouth. What do these statements mean?

5. Comment on Paul's closing statements that describe the damaging effects of sin upon the human community.

No fear of God

Yielding to the Spirit

—Know—

We have learned that the sin of Adam and Eve has affected the entire human race. Are fallen humans essentially evil, or are they essentially good? These kinds of questions relate to the concepts of **total depravity** and **original sin**.

The term **original sin** refers to the fallen, sinful nature that was passed on from Adam to the entire human race. **Total depravity** refers to the extent to which Adam's nature was negatively affected by his sin. It means that every part of human nature (physical and spiritual) was corrupted when Adam rebelled against God. Paul refers to this sin nature as the "flesh," the "old man," the "body of sin," and the "natural man."

Although the Bible mostly refers to sin as an act or deed, it also speaks of sin as a disease or a power that controls the sinner. The prophet Jeremiah writes, "The heart is more deceitful than all else and is desperately sick" (Jeremiah 17:9 NASB). According to the psalmist, we are born with a sinful nature. David states, "Behold, I was brought forth in iniquity, and in sin my mother conceived me" (Psalm 51:5). This scripture does not mean that procreation and childbirth are inherently evil; rather, it means that sinfulness is deeply rooted in human existence and permeates all human life from generation to generation. The corruption of human nature that we call original sin is a lack of righteousness and also a natural tendency toward sin. Thus, it is not only a lack of goodness but is also an active power that leads the human heart toward sin and disobedience.

Original sin and total depravity are manifested in four ways. First, we are born into a state of **unbelief** with no knowledge of God. It follows that without a knowledge of God, we have no love for God. Second, the lack of knowledge leads to a **prideful** idolatry in which we naturally worship ourselves as the center of our lives. We worship ourselves and our own desires. Third, our pride produces **self-will**. As sinners, we do not seek after

God's will but our own will. Fourth, without a love for God, we naturally **love the world**. John writes, "Do not love the world … For all that is in the world—the lust of the flesh, the lust of the eyes, and the pride of life—is not of the Father but is of the world" (1 John 2:15-16). So then, the image of God in humanity has been damaged by unbelief, pride, self-will, and the love of the world in all its aspects.

—Be—

How does this truth transform us? According to John Wesley, original sin is the reason why we must be born again. The new birth is the healing of the disease of sin and the implanting of a new nature that is created in the image of Christ in righteousness and true holiness.

Knowing that "all have sinned" places us all on the same level. Without Christ, we all stand condemned. If we understand that all humanity is suffering from the disease of sin and the corruption of human nature, then we are able to look at our neighbor with compassion and with the love of Christ. Also, the knowledge that we were born in sin should make us all the more thankful that we have been healed of sin's corruption and delivered from sin's power.

—Do—

Take a moment to give thanks to God that He delivered you from the power of darkness. Praise Him that He has cleansed you from all sin.

Let us be imitators of Jesus Christ, who came not to "condemn the world" but to save it (John 3:17). We know that, apart from Christ, the whole world lies in darkness. Let us be the light of God that shines upon the world. Sinners will commit sin, because it is in their fallen nature to do so. Our role is not to continually condemn sinners but to share the gospel with them.

Prayerfully, make a list of sinners with whom you are acquainted. Perhaps you have family members who do not know Christ. Pray for everyone on your list and ask God to give them the grace to call upon the Lord for salvation.

Offer a Prayer

Lord of Life, I praise You. You are the God of my salvation. I thank You that when I was lost, You found me. I was without hope and without peace, but You saved me. I pray that You will transform my view of sinners. Every sinner is a person for whom You died. You died for the Muslim extremists, and You died for the intellectual atheists. I pray that You will reveal Your love and grace to sinners, and I ask You to make me a better witness to the lost. In Jesus' name. Amen.

Day 5

The Penalty of Death

Searching the Scripture

Read Romans 6:23

> For the wages of sin is death, but the gift of God is eternal life in Christ Jesus our Lord.

Read Luke 13:1-5

> There were present at that season some who told Him about the Galileans whose blood Pilate had mingled with their sacrifices. And Jesus answered and said to them, "Do you suppose that these Galileans were worse sinners than all other Galileans, because they suffered such things? "I tell you, no; but unless you repent you will all likewise perish. "Or those eighteen on whom the tower in Siloam fell and killed them, do you think that they were worse sinners than all other men who dwelt in Jerusalem? "I tell you, no; but unless you repent you will all likewise perish."

Read Revelation 20:11-15

> Then I saw a great white throne and Him who sat on it, from whose face the earth and the heaven fled away. And there was found no place for them. And I saw the dead, small and great, standing before God, and books were opened. And another book was opened, which is the Book of Life. And the dead were judged ... And anyone

not found written in the Book of Life was cast into the lake of fire.

Answer the Following Questions:

1. Comment on the statement "the wages of sin is death." How does it relate to our previous studies this week?

2. In Luke 13, what does Jesus mean by the word "perish"?

3. Adam was warned that disobedience would result in death. How does that warning play out in Revelation 20?

Cass into the lake of fire

Yielding to the Spirit

—Know—

Death! Final judgment! A lake burning with fire and brimstone! Eternal destiny! These are sobering scenes for us. We are a generation who tries to avoid such thoughts, choosing instead to focus our attention on more positive and hopeful images. However, because of Adam's sin every human must face death. "And as it is appointed for men to die once, but after this the judgment …" (Hebrews 9:27). The Bible insists that we take seriously the eternal consequences of our present activities. We are making daily choices that will determine our status on Judgment Day.

Those whose names are not written in the Book of Life will be cast into the lake of fire, suffering eternal punishment along with their masters, the devil and the false prophet. The lake of fire is a final and irrevocable doom. It is eternal separation from God.

Death has been passed down to every human being, but what about the children who have not reached the age of accountability? If they die, do they suffer eternal death? Even infants are involved in the guilt of Adam's sin, but this guilt does not lead to eternal punishment. None are lost because of an inherited guilt but only as a result of their own guilt. God assures us that children shall not die for the iniquity of their fathers (Ezekiel 18:17). The atoning work of Christ is sufficient to cover the Adamic guilt that in some sense is mediated even to infants.

—Be—

How does this truth transform us? The certainty of eternal judgment should cause us to examine ourselves in two ways. First, we should examine our own devotion to Jesus Christ. Will our names be written in the book of life? In Revelation, those whose names are not written in the Book of Life are worshipers of the beast (Revelation 13:8). Who are you worshiping? Who are you serving? Second, we should examine our attitude toward the unbelievers. A prominent theme of the Book of Revelation is the "testimony" or "witness" of Jesus Christ. We are His witnesses. God has called us to a mission that has eternal consequences. Our lives, our work, our worship, our teaching, our prayers, our preaching, our passions, our words, and our witness will impact eternity.

—Do—

Go back and read today's Scripture verses again, asking the Holy Spirit to speak to you. Read the Scriptures carefully and prayerfully. Perhaps you will find that there is something you missed before, something the Holy Spirit is wanting to say to you today as He illuminates the inspired Word of God. If so, make note of it in the space below and then use it as a point for prayer today.

Pray a Prayer in Your Own Words

You may wish to write your prayer in the space below.

Group Discussion

Key Scripture — Romans 3:23

"For all have sinned and fall short of the glory of God."

Opening—This is a time of fellowship and sharing about one another's lives.

Prayer—Ask the Lord to make His presence known and to begin the process of transformation into Christ-likeness for each participant.

Testimony—Have two or three group members give a testimony of how God is at work in their lives, whether it is through their daily encounters in this study, or some other way.

Discussion Questions:

1. We normally begin our discussions of salvation with the observation that "all have sinned." However, the Bible begins with God's affirmation of His original creation as "very good." Discuss the importance of recognizing the original inherent goodness of Adam and Eve.

2. Discuss the fact that Adam and Eve were created in the image of God. What does that mean to you?

3. In what way was the image of God marred when Adam sinned? Where do you see fragments or traces of the image of God in humanity today?

4. Go back and read Psalm 51:1-9. How does David describe his sin? How does he illustrate the seriousness of sin?

5. Can you think of a time when you tried to do good but ended up doing what was wrong? Give opportunity for each person in the group to share an example of how every aspect of life has been tainted by sin.

6. Allow each person to share what they remember about their lives as sinners. What was it like to live without God—to suffer the broken relationship with the Creator?

Yielding to the Spirit

If you wish, you might break off into small groups or pair off with someone with whom you feel comfortable sharing. Take a moment to remind each person of the Group Covenant, particularly the statement of confidentiality. Discuss any personal takeaways that you would like your partner to pray about with you. Conclude this conversation by praying for one another. Be attentive to the leading of the Holy Spirit in the use of spiritual gifts. If you do feel led to share a word from the Lord, ask the group leader to come and witness what is being said, so as to provide a reliable witness for all involved.

Week 2

RESTORED RELATIONSHIP

Week 2

Day 1

Everyone Must Repent

DECLARATION OF FAITH

"We Believe . . .

That all have sinned and come short of the glory of God and that repentance is commanded of God for all and necessary for forgiveness of sins."

Words to Hide in Your Heart

Truly, these times of ignorance God overlooked, but now commands all men everywhere to repent (Acts 17:30).

Touching Base

Our focus this week is on the doctrine of repentance as the means to restore the broken relationship with God. Before we can understand how this applies to our lives as people of the Spirit, we must first understand what it means! The term "repent" may be defined as "to change one's way of life as the result of a complete change of thought and attitude with regard to sin and righteousness."

Repentance is the proper response to the convicting power of the Holy Spirit. When the Holy Spirit reveals to us that we have sinned against God, we feel sorrow for our failures and for our offenses. Therefore, the first aspect of repentance is a change of heart.

The feeling of sorrow is followed by a change of mind, in which we believe the gospel. Our thoughts are brought into line with God's thoughts regarding sin, forgiveness, God, Christ, and ourselves.

The change in our minds produces a corresponding change in direction. We turn away from our sins and turn toward God. The apostle Peter declared, "Repent therefore and be converted, that your sins may be blotted out, so that times of refreshing may come from the presence of the Lord" (Acts 3:19).

There is no substitute for repentance, and genuine repentance cannot be imitated. The nature of repentance may be explained further by the following points. First, repentance does not consist of doing good deeds to make up for our failures. We cannot earn our salvation. Repentance is not an attempt to become worthy of forgiveness; it is an admission that we will never be worthy and that we must rely totally upon God's mercy. Second, repentance is not feeling sorry that we were caught. A truly repentant person does not want to be saved in their sins but from their sins. Repentance is a total rejection of our sins. Third, repentance is a rejection of all other gods and a commitment to the God of the Bible as our one and only master. Jesus stated, for example, "You cannot serve God and money" (Matthew 6:24 NIV). Fourth, repentance involves openness and honesty about our sins. We will be forgiven only if we totally confess. The Bible tells us, "If we confess our sins, He is faithful and just to forgive us our sins and to cleanse us from all unrighteousness" (1 John 1:9). Repentance, therefore, does not include bargaining with God, arguing with God, negotiating with God, or rationalizing our sins. Repentance is not making a deal with God; it is total surrender to God's point of view.

Searching the Scripture

Read 2 Timothy 2:25

> … in humility correcting those who are in opposition, if God perhaps will grant them repentance, so that they may know the truth.

Read Mark 1:14-15

> Now after John was put in prison, Jesus came into Galilee, preaching the gospel of the kingdom of God, and saying, "The time is fulfilled, and the kingdom of God is at hand: repent and believe the gospel."

Answer the Following Questions:

1. Can anyone repent on their own, without God's help? NO

2. How does God "grant them repentance"?

   Truth

3. Notice how Jesus combined three ideas: the kingdom of God, repentance, and believing the gospel. How do you think these three things are related?

repentance

Yielding to the Spirit

—Know—

We learned last week that everyone stands guilty before God. None can escape this condemnation except through repentance. Repentance is a turning, a change of direction, based on a change of mind and heart. This change is initiated through the conviction of the Holy Spirit and is necessary for forgiveness. That is, God does not forgive us unless He sees within us a desire to be faithful to Him in the new covenant.

The message of John the Baptist was "Prepare the way of the Lord," and "bear fruits worthy of repentance" (Matthew 3:3-8). The way of the Lord is the way of righteousness, holiness, and love. The call to repentance is a call to restore the moral standard of the way of the Lord. John applied his message to religious leaders, to the common people, to publicans, to soldiers, and to all others who came under his ministry. Everyone was in need of repentance. It is the same today.

—Be—

Do you remember the day when you first repented and turned to God? What stands out about that experience? The most notable aspect of my conversion was the role of the church. I was saved during a revival service where the gospel was preached. The Holy Spirit brought deep conviction to my mind and heart, but I did not know how to respond. Caring Christians gathered around me and guided me through the process of repenting of my sins, believing upon Jesus Christ, and confessing Him as my Savior.

Have you ever prayed with someone as they repented and received Christ as their Savior? We must be open and available to be used of God. Unbelievers need our prayers and our guidance if they are to be born again. We can make a difference in the lives of others if we will show forth a caring and compassionate spirit.

—Do—

Spend some time reflecting on your experience of salvation. You may want to write out your testimony and share it with other people. If the opportunity presents itself, pray with someone and guide them through the process of repentance.

Offer a Prayer

Lord, I thank You that You have provided for us a way of salvation. I realize that I was born in sin and that I lived in sin before You found me. I acknowledge that my sins separated me from You and that I was powerless to make myself better. Thank You for drawing me by Your Spirit. Please help me to care about the lost people who are all around me. Give me the courage and the faith to witness to them about Your love and grace. I pray that You will grant repentance to the lost in my neighborhood. In Jesus' name, I pray. Amen.

Day 2

A Change of Heart

Searching the Scripture

Read Psalm 130

Out of the depths I have cried to You, O LORD;
  Lord, hear my voice!
Let Your ears be attentive
  To the voice of my supplications.
If You, LORD, should mark iniquities,
  O Lord, who could stand?
But there is forgiveness with You,
  That You may be feared.
I wait for the LORD, my soul waits,
  And in His word I do hope.
My soul waits for the Lord
  More than those who watch for the morning—
  Yes, more than those who watch for the morning.
O Israel, hope in the LORD;
  For with the LORD there is mercy,
  And with Him is abundant redemption.
And He shall redeem Israel
  From all his iniquities.

Answer the Following Questions:

1. What kind of emotion is expressed in the words "Out of the depths?

2. What is the meaning of the phrase "who could stand"?

3. What are the different words that the psalmist uses in reference to sin?

4. What are the different words that the psalmist uses in reference to salvation?

Yielding to the Spirit

—Know—

Repentance involves our emotions as our hearts are touched by the Holy Spirit and we begin to feel a sense of sorrow for our sins. The sorrow of broken relationship is expressed in Psalm 130 through the words "out of the depths" (v. 1). All he agony, all the pain, all the guilt, and all the shame is spoken directly to the Lord from within the depths of suffering. A powerful figure of speech, "the depths" brings to mind the feeling of despair and urgency that might overtake a person who is drowning in deep waters with no way of escape (see Psalm 69:15). Here in Psalm 130, the psalmist is drowning in the guilt and alienation brought on by sin (v. 3); therefore, a desperate cry goes out to the Lord, the God of Israel, the God who heard the cries of slaves, brought them out of Egypt, and joined himself to them in covenant.

The psalmist implores God to listen and to hear his prayer. At the end of verse 2, the prayer is revealed to be an appeal for God's mercy or grace. The act of pleading for grace is full of emotion and reveals the psalmist's deep desire for restoration of the covenant relationship with God.

The psalmist, claiming no merit whatever, confesses the universal failure of humanity, and in so doing, confesses his own sinfulness. If God's acceptance of humanity were based upon His observation of iniquities, no one could stand acquitted, including the psalmist. A multitude of iniquities prohibits anyone from standing innocent before God, 'but forgiveness is with' the Lord. The grace of God is the only source of hope. Perhaps the psalmist remembers the Lord's forgiveness of Israel when they built and worshiped the golden calf (Exodus 34:9) or when they grumbled at Kadesh Barnea (Numbers 14:19-20). The Lord is the only source of forgiveness.

—Be—

In Psalm 130, we witness the kind of grief and deep regret that produces genuine repentance. It is the kind of grief that Jesus was referring to when He said, "Blessed are those who mourn, for they shall be comforted" (Matthew 5:4). It is the same kind of grief that Paul talked about when he wrote the following:

> Now I rejoice, not that you were made sorry, but that your sorrow led to repentance. For you were made sorry in a godly manner, that you might suffer loss from us in nothing. For godly sorrow produces repentance leading to salvation, not to be regretted; but the sorrow of the world produces death (2 Corinthians 7:9-10).

The first step in repentance is a change of heart, just as David said, "the sacrifices of God are a broken spirit, a broken and a contrite heart—These, O God, You will not despise" (Psalm 51:17). Through repentance, the relationship between the sinner and God can be restored.

—*Do*—

Repentance is always a personal encounter with God. It originates when God convicts the individual of sin. It is the individual's response to this act of divine grace to correct his/her own way in the fear of God. To those who do not know Christ as Savior, this is a crisis call.

No matter how long we have served the Lord, we should never lose the sense of humility and brokenness that the psalmist displays in Psalm 130. Our righteous deeds do not make us worthy of salvation. Without God's mercy, we would still be lost in our sins.

During this study over the next few weeks, make it a point to begin your daily Bible reading with a simple prayer. Let it become part of your routine as a growing disciple of Jesus Christ who is being transformed into Christlikeness by the work of the Holy Spirit.

Offer a Prayer

Father, I come to You today as a broken vessel. I confess that I need Your grace today just as much as I ever did. As I open Your Word to read today, I open myself to be read by Your Spirit. I present my hungry heart to You and ask You to fill it. Teach me, transform me, complete me, and equip me so that I can serve You more faithfully as I await the coming of our Savior Jesus Christ. In His name, I pray. Amen.

Day 3

A Change of Mind

Searching the Scripture

Read Matthew 21:28-31

> A man had two sons, and he came to the first and said, "Son, go, work today in my vineyard." He answered and said, "I will not," but afterward he regretted it and went. Then he came to the second and said likewise. And he answered and said, "I go, sir," but he did not go. Which of the two did the will of his father? They said to Him, "The first ..."

Read Acts 2:38

> Then Peter said to them, "Repent, and let every one of you be baptized in the name of Jesus Christ for the remission of sins; and you shall receive the gift of the Holy Spirit."

Answer the Following Questions:

1. In Matthew 21, the first son refuses to obey his father, but then he changes his mind. How is this story an illustration of repentance?

2. The second son claimed to be willing, but he did not follow through with his promise. How does he compare to some religious people?

3. In Acts 2, Peter was preaching to the Jewish people, yet he called on them to repent. What does that say about the necessity of repentance for everyone?

Yielding to the Spirit

—Know—

True repentance involves not only the emotions (the heart) but also the mind, attitudes, and will. We should feel sorry for our sins, but we must make the decision to seek forgiveness. Before we can be forgiven, we must believe that Jesus Christ died for our sins. That belief involves a change of mind about sin—it is no longer a small matter; it is dreadful, terrible, and hateful. It involves a change of mind about ourselves—we see ourselves as hopeless without Christ. It involves a change of mind about God—He is holy and righteous, but also loving and merciful.

Repentance is necessary for everyone. As we mentioned briefly last week, Jesus gave the following illustration:

> There were present at that season some who told Him about the Galileans whose blood Pilate had mingled with their sacrifices. And Jesus answered and said to them, "Do you suppose that these Galileans were worse sinners than all other Galileans, because they suffered such things? "I tell you, no; but unless you repent you will all likewise perish. "Or those eighteen on whom the tower in Siloam fell and killed them, do you think that they were worse sinners than all other men who dwelt in Jerusalem? "I tell you, no; but unless you repent you will all likewise perish" (Luke 13:1-5).

Repentance is required for everyone and is necessary for the forgiveness of sins.

—*Be*—

What does it mean for us to say that we believe in repentance? For the true Christian, it means that we take sin seriously, and we do not avoid telling the truth about ourselves. It means that we do not claim to be good or righteous outside of Jesus Christ. To believe in repentance means that we need God's grace. It means that we accept God's mercy as the only way of salvation. To believe in repentance means that we are available to share the gospel with unbelievers and to help them as they seek to repent of their sins and to receive forgiveness.

—*Do*—

When we became a Christian, we changed our minds about God, Christ, sin, and ourselves. We accepted God's will and God's perspective. Are there any areas of life where you have drifted away from God's perspective? Take a moment to prayerfully search your heart. Pray the following prayer as David prayed:

Offer a Prayer

"Search me, O God, and know my heart: try me, and know my thoughts: and see if there be any wicked way in me, and lead me in the way everlasting" (Psalm 139:23-24 KJV). O Lord, I lay all my faults before You, and I surrender to Your will. Let my mind be the mind of Christ. As I study Your Word, please let the Holy Spirit search me and conform me to the image of Jesus Christ. Like the psalmist, I hope in You, and I wait for You more than the watchman waits for the morning. I ask these things in the name of Jesus and for Your glory. Amen.

Day 4

A Change of Direction

Searching the Scripture

Read Luke 15:11-24

> Then He said: "A certain man had two sons. And the younger of them said to his father, 'Father, give me the portion of goods that falls to me.' So he divided to them his livelihood. And not many days after, the younger son gathered all together, journeyed to a far country, and there wasted his possessions with prodigal living ... But when he came to himself, he said, 'How many of my father's hired servants have bread enough and to spare, and I perish with hunger! `I will arise and go to my father, and will say to him, "Father, I have sinned against heaven and before you, and I am no longer worthy to be called your son. Make me like one of your hired servants."' And he arose and came to his father. But when he was still a great way off, his father saw him and had compassion, and ran and fell on his neck and kissed him. And the son said to him, 'Father, I have sinned against heaven and in your sight, and am no longer worthy to be called your son.' But the father said to his servants, 'Bring out the best robe and put it on him ... for this my son was dead and is alive again; he was lost and is found.'"

Answer the Following Questions:

1. The younger son broke the relationship between himself and his father, but eventually he wanted to restore the relationship. Comment on the phrase, "he came to himself."

2. Obviously, the young man was sorry for his sins, but he also exercised his will and admitted the error of his ways. Did he truly repent?

3. Can we say that the young man made a change of direction? What evidence do you see?

Yielding to the Spirit

—Know—

True repentance involves not only a change of heart and a change of mind; it also involves a change of direction. The preaching of Peter included the following command: "Repent therefore and be converted, that your sins may be blotted out" (Acts 3:19). Repentance involves "conversion," which means a change of course or a change of behavior.

On the negative side, repentance is a turning away from the past. When the Ephesians turned to the Lord, they destroyed their books of magic (Acts 19:19) in order to make a clean break from the past. The Thessalonians, likewise, were well-known for their change of direction. Paul says to them,

> Your faith toward God has gone out, so that we do not need to say anything. For they themselves declare concerning us what manner of entry we had to you, and how you turned to God from idols to serve the living and true God, and to wait for His Son from heaven (1 Thessalonians 1:8-10).

Paul commends them for turning away "from idols," an action that indicates genuine repentance on their part. Paul and Barnabas preached to the people of Lystra that they "should turn from these useless things to the living God" (Acts 14:15). As far back as the Old Testament, we read that the wicked should "forsake his way" (Isaiah 55:7), and that Israel should repent and turn away from your idols (Ezekiel 14:6).

On the positive side, repentance is a turning to God. The Thessalonians had "turned to God from idols" with the clear intent of serving God. When Paul preached to king Agrippa, he declared that sinners must "repent, turn to God, and do works befitting repentance" (Acts 26:20).

James is a very practical handbook for living the Christian life. The passage of Scripture in focus today is a good summary of his entire letter. It is a call to actually live out what we say we believe. James accents this so much that some have tried to say that he and Paul disagreed on the issue of faith and works—but that is not true! Both believed in the need for our lives to demonstrate the content of our faith—or in our case, our Declaration of Faith!

—Be—

True repentance is a change of direction, a turning away from things in our past and a turning toward God to serve God and wait for the coming of Jesus. Some people find it difficult to live the Christian life because they have never made a complete change of direction. It is impossible to serve God if we are still hanging on to the past —past sins, past hurts, past disappointments, past desires, past idols, past goals, and past hopes. Transformation will surely follow a clean break from the past.

—Do—

Are you holding on to the past? Are you carrying a grudge? Are you harboring some secret sin? Have you been dishonest in your words or your actions? You must become honest with yourself and honest with God. Choose today to submit every aspect of your life to the authority of God's Word.

Offer a Prayer

Lord, I thank You for the Holy Spirit, who reached into my heart and caused me to repent of my sins. I made a change of heart, a change of mind, and a change of direction. However, I admit that the Enemy has tempted me to pick up things from the past. I choose now to release all the past and count it as trash, so that I might hold fast to Your hand. I need Your mercy, grace, and strength to walk faithfully in newness of life. Just as Christ gave His all for me, I desire to give my all for Him. In Jesus' name. Amen.

Day 5

The Penitent Life

Searching the Scripture

Read Revelation 2:1-5

> "To the angel of the church of Ephesus write, 'These things says He who holds the seven stars in His right hand, who walks in the midst of the seven golden lampstands: I know your works, your labor, your patience, and that you cannot bear those who are evil. And you have tested those who say they are apostles and are not, and have found them liars; and you have persevered and have patience, and have labored for My name's sake and have not become weary. Nevertheless I have this against you, that you have left your first love. Remember therefore from where you have fallen; repent and do the first works, or else I will come to you quickly and remove your lampstand from its place—unless you repent.'"

Answer the Following Questions:

1. Jesus tells John to write a prophetic message to the church at Ephesus. What words of affirmation does Jesus speak to this church?

2. What is the one failure of the church at Ephesus?

3. How can the church correct its error?

4. Comment on the necessity of repentance for the church at Ephesus.

Yielding to the Spirit

—Know—

We normally associate repentance with the initial experience of conversion, and we should. However, the Bible teaches us that repentance is also needed in the Church and in the lives of individual Christians. The repentance called for in Revelation 2:5 is not the repentance of unbelievers who are turning to God for the first time; it is the repentance of believers.

In the New Testament, the call to repentance is addressed to the unbeliever (Acts 17:30), to the Jew (Acts 2:38), and to the Christian alike (Revelation 2:5); and for each group, the Greek word for "repent" is the same (*metanoeo*). True repentance includes the act of confessing one's sins, whether one is an unbeliever (Mark 1:5), a Jew (Matthew 3:2-7), or a Christian (1 John 1:9).

In addition to initial repentance [at conversion], repentance is a grace which is to be practiced throughout one's life in Christ. Two factors make repentance necessary for the Christian. The first is the believer's growth in grace and knowledge. As the believers become more mature, they become aware of shortcomings that should be laid aside (Hebrews 12:1). The second is the occasion of known sin in the life of the believer (1 John 1:9). Every Christian should be careful to avoid falling into any of the works of the flesh (Galatians 5:16-26). If we discover a root of pride, bitterness, envy, or any other work of the flesh, we must immediately repent.

—Be—

Rather than a one-time event, salvation is understood to be a journey that involves both crisis and development. As we mature on our journey, regular searching of the heart and repenting should be a way of living in Christ. It is essential for renewal, and life that is not in continual renewal will die. John Wesley, for example, urged his followers to examine themselves daily and to repent of any sins of commission or omission.

Corporate repentance is a significant topic that shows up in Scripture (for example, Psalms 130:7-8 and Joel 2). Although individual repentance is demanded by Scripture, corporate repentance is called for with equal severity and should be practiced by the Church. After all, in his prophetic messages to the churches of Asia Minor, Jesus seven times calls for repentance (Revelation 2:5, 5, 16, 21, 22; 3:3, 19).

The Scripture urges us to help each other repent. James writes, "Confess your trespasses to one another, and pray for one another, that you may be healed. The effective, fervent prayer of a righteous man avails much" (James 5:16).

—Do—

The ongoing life of repentance is facilitated by several Pentecostal practices, including footwashing, the Lord's Supper, and the altar call that may follow preaching. Footwashing is the sacrament that speaks most directly to post-conversion sin, but the Lord's Supper also provides the opportunity for believers to 'examine' themselves (1 Corinthians 11:28) and to repent of any known sin. Repentance can also be a response to the preaching of the Word of God, as the minister gives opportunity for the congregation to pray at the altar or to kneel at their seats and seek the face of God.

You may want to schedule a regular prayer time when you will ask God to reveal any areas of your life that are unpleasing to Him. Then you can repent and seek God's strength for victory over these areas.

Pray a Prayer in Your Own Words

Make a list of the most troublesome temptations that you face, and compose a personal prayer of repentance that will empower you to put those things behind you.

Group Discussion

Key Scripture—Galatians 6:1-3

> Brethren, if a man is overtaken in any trespass, you who are spiritual restore such a one in a spirit of gentleness, considering yourself lest you also be tempted. Bear one another's burdens, and so fulfill the law of Christ. For if anyone thinks himself to be something, when he is nothing, he deceives himself.

Opening—This is a time of fellowship and sharing about one another's lives.

Prayer—Ask the Lord to make His presence known and to begin the process of transformation into Christlikeness for each participant.

Testimony—Have two or three group members give a testimony of how God is at work in their lives, whether it is through their daily encounters in this study, or some other way.

Discussion Questions:

1. Discuss your church's policies and practices for dealing with fellow Christians who have fallen into sin.

2. Are there ways that your church could do a better job of lifting up those who have fallen?

3. How important is confidentiality in the process of restoring a fallen brother or sister

4. Discuss some of the most common areas where Christians give in to temptation.

5. Let each person share a Scripture regarding victory over temptation. How can we help each other be victorious?

Yielding to the Spirit

Group members should pair off with someone with whom they feel comfortable sharing. Take a moment to remind them of the Group Covenant, particularly the statement of confidentiality. Discuss any personal takeaways that you would like your partner to pray about with you. Conclude this conversation by praying for one another. Be attentive to the leading of the Holy Spirit in the use of spiritual gifts. If you do feel led to share a word from the Lord, ask the group leader to come and witness what is being said, so as to provide a reliable witness for all involved.

Week 3

LIVING IN CHRIST

DECLARATION OF FAITH

◆◆◆◆◆◆◆

"We believe . . .

That justification, regeneration, and the new birth are wrought by faith in the blood of Jesus Christ."

Week 3

Day 1

Forgiven

DECLARATION OF FAITH

"We Believe....

That justification, regeneration, and the new birth are wrought by faith in the blood of Jesus Christ."

Words to Hide in Your Heart

But God demonstrates His own love toward us, in that while we were still sinners, Christ died for us. Much more then, having now been justified by His blood, we shall be saved from wrath through Him. For if when we were enemies we were reconciled to God through the death of His Son, much more, having been reconciled, we shall be saved by His life (Romans 5:8-10).

Touching Base

Our focus this week is on the doctrine of conversion, which is expressed in the teaching that **justification, regeneration, and the new birth are wrought by faith in the blood of Jesus Christ**. This statement makes it clear that we are saved by grace through faith. Our relationship to God is restored only because of the sacrificial death of Christ. It is His merit that redeems us. This restored relationship to God is entered into and maintained by faith in Christ, not by our works.

In this week's study, we will look at two aspects of our salvation: justification and regeneration (also called the new birth). The word "justification" means to show why someone is in the right. To use biblical terminology, it is the declaring of someone to be "righteous." Without the grace of God, however, none of us are in the right or righteous—we are all condemned as sinners. Paul writes, "There is none righteous, no, not one" (Romans 3:10). When we come to God in faith, He forgives our past sins because of the sacrifice of Jesus on the cross, and He declares us to be righteous, restoring us to a right relationship with Him. We are "justified freely by His grace" (Romans 3:24). Justification is equivalent to a pardon. God knows that we are guilty, but He pardons us so that we no longer suffer the punishment for our sins. We are justified, not because of any good works that we have done, but because of our faith in Jesus Christ. We are set free by God's grace, and His forgiveness restores our broken relationship to God; and we have peace with God.

The word "regeneration" means to be reborn. Regeneration is God's gift of eternal life to us who were spiritually dead. To be regenerated is also known as being "born again," "born of God," and "born of the Spirit." This impartation of life enables us to love God and obey God. Therefore, regeneration frees us from the **power** of sin, in contrast to justification, which frees us from the **guilt** of sin. Justification is something that God does **for** us, and regeneration is something that God does **in** us. Justification and regeneration go together—it would be impossible to have one without the other. We experience both justification and regeneration as instantaneous and essentially simultaneous. As soon as God forgives us, He imparts new life into our souls.

Searching the Scripture

Read Romans 3:24, 28

> Being **justified** freely by His grace through the redemption that is in Christ Jesus ... Therefore we conclude that a man is **justified by faith** apart from the deeds of the law.

Read Titus 3:5

> Not by works of righteousness which we have done, but according to His mercy He saved us, through the washing of **regeneration** and renewing of the Holy Spirit.

Read 1 Peter 1:23

> . . . having been **born again**, not of corruptible seed but incorruptible, through the word of God which lives and abides forever.

Read Colossians 1:14

> . . . in whom we have redemption through **His blood**, the forgiveness of sins.

Answer the Following Questions:

1. After reading Romans 3:24 and 28, explain the relationship between faith, grace, and justification.

   Our faith & His Grace

2. In light of Titus 3:5, reflect on the combination of "regeneration" and the "renewing" of the Spirit.

3. According to 1 Peter 1:23, what is the role of the Word of God in the new birth?
   to be born again

4. According to Colossians 1:14, what is the basis for our "redemption" and the "forgiveness" of our sins? Jesus Blood

Yielding to the Spirit

—Know—

When speaking about salvation, the Bible uses a rich variety of words and symbols, each one emphasizing a specific benefit of God's grace. Through faith in the blood of Christ, we are justified (Romans 5:9); we are redeemed (Ephesians 1:7); we are forgiven (Hebrews 9:22); we are converted (Matthew 18:3); we are adopted (Galatians 4:5); we are born again (John 1:13); we are cleansed (Hebrews 9:14); we are reconciled to God (Colossians 1:20); we are delivered (Romans 5:9); we have eternal life (John 6:54); we are healed (John 12:40); we are washed (Revelation 1:5); we are made new creatures in Christ (2 Corinthians 5:17).

—Be—

In these mighty acts of salvation, God transforms sinners into saints. He restores the broken relationship between God and humanity. He restores in us the image of God that had been marred by sin. He rescues us from the kingdom of darkness and brings us into the kingdom of God (Colossians 1:13). He makes us His children, part of His family (John 1:12).

—Do—

As you prepare to go through each day for the remainder of this study, begin with the following prayer.

Offer a Prayer

Lord I thank You for the grace that You have extended to me through Jesus Christ. I was lost, but now I am found. I was blind, but now I can see. It is my desire to have a better understanding of the way of salvation. I pray that You will speak to me this week through Your Word. I pray the prayer of Paul for the Ephesians, that You will give to me the spirit of wisdom and revelation in the knowledge of You, that the eyes of my understanding might be enlightened; that I may know what is the hope of Your calling, and what are the riches of the glory of Your inheritance, and what is the exceeding greatness of Your power toward us who believe, according to the working of Your mighty power, which You worked in Christ when You raised Him from the dead and seated Him at Your right hand in the heavenly places. In Jesus' name I pray. Amen.

Day 2

Declared Righteous

Searching the Scripture

Read Romans 5:1-10

> Therefore, having been justified by faith, we have peace with God through our Lord Jesus Christ, through whom also we have access by faith into this grace in which we stand, and rejoice in hope of the glory of God … For when we were still without strength, in due time Christ died for the ungodly. For scarcely for a righteous man will one die; yet perhaps for a good man someone would even dare to die. But God demonstrates His own love toward us, in that while we were still sinners, Christ died for us. Much more then, having now been justified by His blood, we shall be saved from wrath through Him. For if when we were enemies we were reconciled to God through the death of His Son, much more, having been reconciled, we shall be saved by His life.

Answer the Following Questions:

1. How do we find peace with God?

   By faith thru Jesus

2. How do we gain access to grace?

   By faith

3. For whom did Christ die?

   for all

4. What was our relationship to God before we were reconciled to Him?

Yielding to the Spirit

—Know—

Justification became an important word for Saul of Tarsus when, on the road to Damascus, he met Christ in a vision (Acts 9:1-22). Saul had been busy persecuting Christians, throwing them in prison and even killing some of them (Acts 22:4), but when he met Jesus, everything changed. The persecutor became a prophet; the murderer became a minister; the agitator became an apostle. Paul learned that justification is pardon, and he wrote "Christ Jesus came into the world to save sinners, of whom I am chief" (1 Timothy 1:15). He learned that justification is forgiveness; and it is receiving the gift of righteousness. Justification and righteousness come from the same root words in the original biblical languages. To be justified is to be given the righteousness of God by the Spirit of God (Romans 3:22). Paul had thought he was righteous (Philippians 3:4-8); he had thought he was doing what was right; but only in his transformation on the Damascus Road was he made righteous. Only through Christ did Paul receive the "righteousness which is from God by faith" (Philippians 3:9). Before he met Christ, Paul had lived under the burden of judgment, but after Paul surrendered to Christ, he was no longer guilty, no longer condemned (Romans 8:1). He learned that when we are "justified by faith, we have peace with God" (Romans 5:1).

—Be—

Justification is more than a theory or a doctrine. It is more than a theological point for discussion. God calls out Abraham and gives him the promise of children and the land of Canaan (Genesis 12:1-3). To Abraham, therefore, justification means family, home, and a future for his children; it means that God's promises would be fulfilled. God "justifies the ungodly by faith" (Romans 4:5), and Abraham "believed God, and it was accounted to him for righteousness" (Romans 4:3). Justification is of vital interest to Zacchaeus, a man known by everyone to be a sinner. Because Jesus is "just and the justifier of the one who has faith" in Him (Romans 3:26), Zacchaeus hears Jesus say, "Today salvation has come to this house" (Luke 19:2-9). To the thief who hangs dying on a cross, justification is a genuine concern. To this wicked man, whose last breath is a plea for forgiveness, justification means being snatched from the flames of hell that are licking at his feet. Because God justifies sinners, the thief hears Jesus say, "Today you will be with Me in Paradise" (Luke 23:43).

—*Do*—

Because we are saved by grace, we have no room for boasting, no room for self-righteousness. We live and work together in gratitude for God's grace that has been poured out on us individually and communally. During this study over the next few weeks, continue to pray this prayer of thanksgiving for God's saving grace.

Offer a Prayer

Heavenly Father, I give thanks to You for the gift of eternal life in Jesus Christ. Through Christ, I come to You with humble but confident faith. I pray that I might not lose heart because of the testing of my faith. I bow before You, my Father, and ask that You would strengthen me through Your Spirit in the inner man; that Christ would dwell in my heart by faith; that I would be rooted and grounded in love; that I may be able to comprehend the depths of Your love, which passes knowledge; and that I may be filled with Your Holy Spirit. You are able to do exceedingly, abundantly above all that I can ask or think. To You I give all the glory by Christ Jesus. Amen.

Day 3

Born Again

Searching the Scripture

Read John 3:3-5

> Jesus answered and said to him, "Most assuredly, I say to you, unless one is **born again**, he cannot see the kingdom of God … unless one is born of water and the Spirit, he cannot enter the kingdom of God."

Read 1 Peter 1:3

> Blessed be the God and Father of our Lord Jesus Christ, who according to His abundant mercy has **begotten us again** to a living hope through the resurrection of Jesus Christ from the dead.

Read 1 Peter 1:23

> having been **born again**, not of corruptible seed but incorruptible, through the word of God which lives and abides forever.

Answer the Following Questions:

1. In John 3:3-5, Jesus explains the requirement for entering the kingdom of God. What is that requirement?

   must be born again

2. How do God's mercy and Christ's resurrection factor into the new birth?

   Begotten us to live in Hope

3. How does the "word of God" factor into the new birth?

   lives and abides forever

Yielding to the Spirit

—Know—

In the Book of Acts, we read that Philip the evangelist was guided by the Holy Spirit to talk to a man from Ethiopia. The Ethiopian experienced the new birth as he was riding in his chariot and reading the prophecy of Isaiah which says, "He was led as a lamb to the slaughter, and as a sheep before its shearers is silent, so He opened not His mouth" (Isaiah 53:7). The Ethiopian asked, "Of whom does the prophet say this?" And, Philip the evangelist began at that Scripture and preached about Jesus. The Ethiopian believed the Scripture and was born again by the Holy Spirit (Acts 8:27-39). He learned that to be born again is to have a new origin and a new nature by the Word of God (1 Peter 1:23), to be recreated in the image of God, to have a fresh start with God and a fresh start in living by the Spirit of God (John 3:3-7). (The words regeneration and new birth have the same meaning. For example, in Titus 3:5, some translations read regeneration, but others read new birth). To be born again is to experience the restoration of the image of God, to be as guiltless as a newborn baby. In the symbolism of Israel's exodus from Egyptian bondage, to be born again is to pass through the waters of birth like Israel passed through the Red Sea. After passing through the Sea, Israel began a new walk with their Savior; and after passing through the waters of the new birth, the Ethiopian eunuch entered into the new covenant (Jeremiah 31:31; Hebrews 12:24) and set out on the life of faith as part of the family of God (Galatians 3:26).

—Be—

How does the truth of regeneration affect our daily lives? To be born again is to be given new life by the Holy Spirit. This new life is more than an extension of the old life or an improvement of the old life. This new life is the life of God himself given to us in the body and blood of Jesus (John 6:53). In fact, the old life is not really life at all; it is death (John 5:24). To be born again is to have new life that is given and sustained by the Word of God, a life that can live victoriously over sin and the devil (1 John 3:9-10). Those who have been born again cannot be hurt by the second death (Revelation 2:11). Regarding the person who is born again, God has a final word to say: "He who overcomes shall inherit all things; and I will be his God and he shall be My son" (Revelation 21:7).

—Do—

In what ways has the new birth made a difference in your life? Briefly describe your experience in two or three sentences on this page.

Offer a Prayer

Heavenly Father, I thank You for finding me and giving me new spiritual life through Jesus Christ. Because I have been born of God, I now can love You freely and I can love other people genuinely. You have filled my life with goodness; therefore, I will praise You forever.

As I think about Your influence in my life, I realize that I have much room for improvement. I submit myself to the work of the Holy Spirit and ask that You form and shape me according to Your will. I desire to be like Christ, and I believe that You can complete the work that You have begun in me. In Jesus' name. Amen.

Day 4

A Child of God

Searching the Scripture

Read Romans 8:14-17

> For as many as are led by the Spirit of God, these are sons of God. For you did not receive the spirit of bondage again to fear, but you received the Spirit of adoption by whom we cry out, "Abba, Father." The Spirit Himself bears witness with our spirit that we are children of God, and if children, then heirs—heirs of God and joint heirs with Christ, if indeed we suffer with Him, that we may also be glorified together.

Answer the Following Questions:

1. What does it mean for us to be led by the Spirit of God?

2. Explain the contrast between the "spirit of bondage" and the "Spirit of adoption."

3. As children of God, we are heirs of God. What kinds of things do we inherit from God?

Peace
all things
eternal life
Escape of Hell

Yielding to the Spirit

—Know—

When you are born again, you become a child of God, and God wants you to have assurance that you belong to Him. He wants you to "know that you have eternal life" (1 John 5:13). But how can we know that we have been born again? First, there is an inner witness of our spirit: "He who believes in the Son of God has the witness in himself" (1 John 5:10). Second, there is the witness of the Holy Spirit: "The Spirit Himself bears witness with our spirit that we are children of God" (Romans 8:16). The witness of our own spirit comes from our conscience. The witness of the Holy Spirit comes directly from God. We do not arrive at this assurance through a process of reasoning or inference; it is just something that we know.

The assurance that we have been reborn comes also from the changes that happen in our lives as a result of becoming "partakers of the divine nature" (2 Peter 1:4). The greatest mark of the new birth is love—the love of God is placed in our hearts by the Holy Spirit (Romans 5:5). No longer will we love ourselves more than anything else. As soon as we become children of God, we will sense a deep love for God and love for people. Not only do we love God, but we love God's teachings, and we have a desire to obey God's commandments.

—*Be*—

How does this truth transform us? How does it affect our daily lives? John explains the place of love within the children of God:

> Beloved, let us love one another, for love is of God; and everyone who loves is born of God and knows God. He who does not love does not know God, for God is love. In this the love of God was manifested toward us, that God has sent His only begotten Son into the world, that we might live through Him. In this is love, not that we loved God, but that He loved us and sent His Son to be the propitiation for our sins. Beloved, if God so loved us, we also ought to love one another. No one has seen God at any time. If we love one another, God abides in us, and His love has been perfected in us. By this we know that we abide in Him, and He in us, because He has given us of His Spirit (1 John 4:7-13).

—Do—

Do you have assurance within your own heart that you are a child of God? Does the Holy Spirit dwell within you? Do you love God and your neighbor? Do you enjoy serving God and worshiping God? We all have our ups and downs, our good days and our bad days. We have not "arrived" yet; we are all in the process of growing. Perhaps you should make a list of a few areas of your life where you could use improvement, and pray for God's help in those areas.

Offer a Prayer

Heavenly Father, I join with David to pray this prayer:

> Bless the LORD, O my soul; And all that is within me, bless His holy name! Bless the LORD, O my soul, and forget not all His benefits: who forgives all your iniquities, who heals all your diseases, who redeems your life from destruction, who crowns you with lovingkindness and tender mercies, who satisfies your mouth with good things, so that your youth is renewed like the eagle's. … He has not dealt with us according to our sins, nor punished us according to our iniquities. For as the heavens are high above the earth, so great is His mercy toward those who fear Him; as far as the east is from the west, so far has He removed our transgressions from us. As a father pities his children, so the LORD pities those who fear

> Him. For He knows our frame; He remembers that we are dust (Psalm 103:1-16).

I thank You that You have made me one of Your children and that You have placed Your Spirit within me. I thank You for new life through Jesus Christ. In Jesus' name. Amen.

Day 5

Indwelt by the Spirit

Searching the Scripture

Read Ezekiel 36:25-28

> Then I will sprinkle clean water on you, and you shall be clean; I will cleanse you from all your filthiness and from all your idols. I will give you a new heart and put a new spirit within you; I will take the heart of stone out of your flesh and give you a heart of flesh. I will put My Spirit within you and cause you to walk in My statutes, and you will keep My judgments and do them. Then you shall dwell in the land that I gave to your fathers; you shall be My people, and I will be your God.

Answer the Following Questions:

1. In Ezekiel 36, God is speaking to Israel regarding the new covenant in Jesus Christ. Six times, God says, "I will …." Make a list of the six things that God will do.

2. How does the combination of "new heart" and "new spirit" relate to what we have already learned about regeneration?

3. What are the stated results of having God's Spirit within us?

Yielding to the Spirit

—Know—

We have talked about the effects of justification, and regeneration (new birth). Justification is the act of forgiveness that restores our covenant relationship to God. We are freed from guilt and are declared to be righteous. Regeneration is the new birth, which implants new life in us and partially restores the image of God in us. The strength to walk with God in the restored relationship and the sustenance of the new life within us are provided by the Holy Spirit, who comes to dwell in our hearts when we become a Christian (Romans 5:9). To be born of God is to be born of the Spirit (John 3:5-6).

Before His crucifixion, Jesus promised the disciples that the Holy Spirit would live within them. Jesus said,

> And I will pray the Father, and He will give you another Helper, that He may abide with you forever—the Spirit of truth, whom the world cannot receive, because it neither sees Him nor knows Him; but you know Him, for He dwells with you and will be in you (John 14:16-17).

After the crucifixion and resurrection of Jesus, the Holy Spirit was poured out on the disciples. Then, when Peter preached to the crowd, he explained that the promise of Jesus was meant for everyone who becomes a Christian:

> Then Peter said to them, "Repent, and let every one of you be baptized in the name of Jesus Christ for the remission of sins; and you shall receive the gift of the Holy Spirit" (Acts 2:38).

—Be—

How does the indwelling of the Spirit transform us? What are the effects of the Holy Spirit upon our lives? Two passages of Scripture elaborate on the role of the Holy Spirit in the life of the believer. In the Gospel of John, Jesus declares that the Spirit will guide believers into the truth, tell us things to come, and glorify Jesus!

> However, when He, the Spirit of truth, has come, He will **guide you into all truth**; ... and He will **tell you things to come**. He will **glorify Me**, for He will take of what is Mine and declare it to you (John 16:13-14).

Paul states a similar point in his letter to the Romans:

> Likewise the Spirit also helps in our weaknesses. For we do not know what we should pray for as we ought, but the Spirit Himself makes intercession for us with groanings which cannot be uttered. Now He who searches the hearts knows what the mind of the Spirit is, because He makes intercession for the saints according to the will of God (Romans 8:26-27).

This second Scripture passage describes how the Holy Spirit helps us in our prayers by making up for our limited knowledge. The Spirit guides us to pray according to the will of God. Have you experienced these benefits of the Holy Spirit in your own life?

—Do—

Go back and reread today's Scripture verses, asking the Holy Spirit to turn on the light. Read them carefully and prayerfully. Perhaps you will find that there is something you missed before, something the Holy Spirit is wanting to say to you as He illuminates the inspired Word of God. If so, make note of it in the space below and then use it as a point for prayer today.

Pray a Prayer in Your Own Words

You may wish to write your prayer in the space below.

Group Discussion

Key Scripture—Romans 5:8-10

> But God demonstrates His own love toward us, in that while we were still sinners, Christ died for us. Much more then, having now been justified by His blood, we shall be saved from wrath through Him. For if when we were enemies we were reconciled to God through the death of His Son, much more, having been reconciled, we shall be saved by His life

Opening—This is a time of fellowship and sharing about one another's lives.

Prayer—Ask the Lord to make His presence known and to begin the process of transformation into Christlikeness for each participant.

Testimony—Have two or three group members give a testimony of how God is at work in their lives, whether it is through their daily encounters in this study, or some other way.

Discussion Questions:

1. Let each person share the testimony of their conversion.

2. Discuss the similarities and differences of the testimonies that you have heard.

3. How do your testimonies compare to the conversion stories of the Samaritans (Acts 8:5-17), the Ethiopian (Acts 8:29-39), and Saul (Acts 9:1-18)?

4. The Scripture passage above (Romans 5:8-10) talks about being "reconciled to God." Discuss with the group the meaning of reconciliation with God.

5. Discuss the idea of the new birth. What were the most immediate changes that you experienced when you were born of God?

Yielding to the Spirit

Group members should pair off with someone with whom they feel comfortable sharing. Take a moment to remind them of the Group Covenant, particularly the statement of confidentiality. Discuss any personal takeaways that you would like your partner to pray about with you. Conclude this conversation by praying for one another. Be attentive to the leading of the Holy Spirit in the use of spiritual gifts. If you do feel led to share a word from the Lord, ask the group leader to come and witness what is being said, so as to provide a reliable witness for all involved.

Week 4

LIVING BY FAITH

Week 4

Day 1

Redeemed by the Blood

DECLARATION OF FAITH

"We Believe....

That justification, regeneration, and the new birth are wrought by faith in the blood of Jesus Christ."

Words to Hide in Your Heart

In Him we have redemption through His blood, the forgiveness of sins, according to the riches of His grace (Ephesians 1:7).

Touching Base

We have discussed the meaning of justification and regeneration, both of which are actions that God does. We do not justify ourselves, and we do not regenerate ourselves. Justification is the forgiveness that God does **for** us, and regeneration is the new life that God puts **in** us. This week we will discuss **faith** and the **blood of Jesus Christ**. Both justification and regeneration are gifts of grace that are given to us when we confess our faith in the atoning, sacrificial death of Jesus. The apostle Paul states, "if you confess with your mouth the Lord Jesus and believe in your heart that God has raised Him from the dead, you will be saved" (Romans 10:9).

Stated simply, faith is belief in the gospel of Jesus Christ, trust in God, and commitment to God in the new covenant. The facts of the gospel must be believed; but we must go beyond believing, for even the demons believe (James 2:19). Saving faith includes the act of trusting God with our salvation and a commitment to serve God. Salvation by faith alone means that we are not able to earn our salvation by any number of good works. Paul writes that it is "not by works of righteousness which we have done, but according to His mercy He saved us" (Titus 3:5). Paul states further, "For by grace you have been saved through faith, and that not of yourselves; it is the gift of God, not of works, lest anyone should boast" (Ephesians 2:8-9).

In its fullest sense, the blood of Jesus represents the entire life and death of Jesus who gave Himself for humanity. The sacrifice of Jesus is described by Paul:

> Who, being in the form of God, did not consider it robbery to be equal with God, but made Himself of no reputation, taking the form of a bondservant, and coming in the likeness of men. And being found in appearance as a man, He humbled Himself and became obedient to the point of death, even the death of the cross (Philippians 2:6-8).

Every part of Jesus' mission was an act of sacrificial service that contributes to our salvation. He humbled Himself to be born as a human being. He suffered hunger, cold, rejection, and pain. He suffered the attack of every kind of temptation but lived a sinless life. Finally, He gave His life for us willingly on the cross. He is the "Lamb slain from the foundation of the world" (Revelation 13:8).

Searching the Scripture

Read Luke 22:19-20

> And He took bread, gave thanks and broke it, and gave it to them, saying, "This is My body which is given for you; do this in remembrance of Me." Likewise He also took the cup after supper, saying, "This cup is the new covenant in My blood, which is shed for you."

Read 1 Peter 1:18-19

> knowing that you were not redeemed with corruptible things, like silver or gold, from your aimless conduct

received by tradition from your fathers, but with the precious blood of Christ, as of a lamb without blemish and without spot (1 Peter 1:18-19).

Answer the Following Questions:

1. Why are we asked to consume the body and blood of Jesus?

2. In the Old Testament, the firstborn were redeemed with silver. Why can't we just pay a fee and be saved?

3. What does it mean that Christ was "without blemish and without spot"?

Yielding to the Spirit

—Know—

The Old Testament story of the Passover (Exodus 12) foreshadowed the death of Jesus. Hurriedly and fearfully they prepared their evening meal. This was no ordinary meal; it was the Lord's Passover. The Lord said He would come down that night and destroy the firstborn of Egypt. If the Israelites were to be saved, they must follow Moses' instructions to the letter. They must slaughter the lamb, being careful not to break any of its bones, and they must spread the blood of the lamb on their doorposts and lintel. "When I see the blood," the Lord promised, "I will pass over you." At midnight the Lord came down as He had warned, and only the Israelites were saved. The next morning, while the Egyptians were mourning the death of their firstborn, God led His people out of bondage; and they set out for the Promised Land, having been saved by the blood of the lamb (Exodus 12:1-51).

The exodus from Egypt is the prophetic model for all of God's saving acts, including His greatest act of salvation that came centuries later. On the banks of the Jordan River, as Jesus of Nazareth approaches, we hear the proclamation of John the Baptist, "Behold! The Lamb of God who takes away the sin of the world!" (John 1:29).

—Be—

In the Book of Revelation, the great multitude who stand before the throne of God have "washed their robes and made them white in the blood of the Lamb" (Revelation 7:14). Peter says that we are not redeemed with silver and gold but "with the precious blood of Christ, as of a lamb without blemish and without spot" (1 Peter 1:19). Our salvation comes not by good works but by faith in the blood of the lamb that was slain (Romans 3:23-25). In the Book of Revelation, there is a clear distinction between the people of God and the people of the world who worship the power and wealth of the "beast." Is there a distinction today between Christians and unbelievers? Are our values different? Do we live differently? Do we spend our money differently? Do we treat others with respect? Do we help the needy?

—Do—

If you were on trial for being a Christian, what evidence could be used to show that you are a believer? After thinking about this question for a few minutes. Make a list of ways that you want your life to change for the better.

Offer a Prayer

Heavenly Father, I thank You that You loved the world enough to send Your son to be our Savior. Lord Jesus, I thank You for the profound sacrifice that You made in becoming a man, living among us, and dying for us. I repent for any times that I did not appreciate Your grace. I pray that You will help me to be more aware of the magnitude of Your love and that You will help me to share that love with others. I ask all of these things in Jesus' name. Amen.

Day 2

The Grace of God

Searching the Scripture

Read Ephesians 2:8-9

> For by grace you have been saved through faith, and that not of yourselves; it is the gift of God, not of works, lest anyone should boast.

Answer the Following Questions:

1. How do grace and faith work together? Is grace given where there is no faith?

2. Is a gift something that is earned, or is it given freely?

3. What are some ways that people try to work their way into God's favor?

Yielding to the Spirit

—Know—

The word "grace" means "favor," and theologically, grace is the free and undeserved favor of God that He shows to us when He forgives our sins and bestows blessings upon us. As we learned earlier, all have sinned, and no one is worthy of God's favor. Without Christ, all humanity is alienated from God and under the penalty of death. However, because of Christ's work, God acts differently toward humanity and extends His grace.

When we talk about grace, it is most often within the context of the conversion experience. We think of Paul's statement, "for by grace you have been saved through faith" (Ephesians 2:8). However, the grace of God is at work in all stages of life: (1) before we hear the gospel, (2) when we receive the gospel and repent, and (3) after we become a believer. First, it is the grace of God that enables us to turn to God. Without God's grace, we would be unable to respond to the good news of Jesus and repent of our sins. Before we came to know Christ, we were spiritually dead, and we did not have the ability to know God or love God. We did not even have the capacity to repent. Prevenient grace (or preceding grace) is the favor that God shows to us by awakening our consciences and giving us the power to accept the gospel and repent of our sins.

Second, if we cooperate with God at that point by believing on the Lord and repenting of our sins, then God's grace is applied to us in forgiveness. His saving grace opens the floodgates of divine blessing, and we are justified, born again, and given eternal life through the Holy Spirit. Grace produces a real transformation in the human soul. Grace in the context of regeneration is the salvific strength of God made available to all who believe.

Third, the grace of God gives us the ability to serve God faithfully. As long as we continue to remain in Christ by trusting Him alone for our righteousness, we will continue to live in the favor of God. Regarding his own Christian service, Paul writes, "But by the grace of God I am what I am, and His grace toward me was not in vain; but I labored more abundantly than they all, yet not I, but the grace of God which was with me" (1 Corinthians 15:10). Although Paul claims to have worked harder than the other apostles, he admits that all his work is accomplished through grace, not through his own strength. Later on, Paul reveals that God had given him assurance regarding the power of grace. The Lord said to Paul, "My grace is sufficient for you, for My strength is made perfect in weakness" (2 Corinthians 12:9). Even after we become a Christian, we do not earn God's favor by our good works. Yes, God is pleased by our good works, and He expects us to live faithfully in fellowship with Him; but His acceptance of us continues to rest upon our faith in Jesus Christ as our righteousness.

—Be—

If we are saved by grace, then does it matter if we continue to sin after we become a Christian? The apostle Paul asked that question, "Shall we continue in sin that grace may abound?" His answer was clearly, NO! Paul writes, "Certainly not! How shall we who died to sin live any longer in it?" (Romans 6:1-2). John Wesley explains that one element of grace is the power of God that liberates from the awful domination of sin. Grace, therefore, is an infusion that produces a real, inherent change in the human soul. The grace that comes to us by way of the new birth is the strength of God made available to all who believe. It is empowerment by the Holy Spirit for obedience to Christ.

—Do—

Read the following Scripture passage and meditate on it for a few minutes. Think about the concept of God's abundant grace as it intersects with the Christian's responsibility to love God and love one's neighbor.

> For the grace of God that brings salvation has appeared to all men, teaching us that, denying ungodliness and worldly lusts, we should live soberly, righteously, and godly in the present age, looking for the blessed hope and

glorious appearing of our great God and Savior Jesus Christ, who gave Himself for us, that He might redeem us from every lawless deed and purify for Himself His own special people, zealous for good works (Titus 2:11-14).

Offer a Prayer

Almighty God and Heavenly Father, I come before You today in need of Your grace. Your grace is always sufficient for whatever I need. In my weakness, I need Your grace. In my failures, I need Your grace. Even in my successes, I need Your grace to prevent me from exalting myself. All of my boasting is in Your grace, because it is Your grace that has created everything in me that is good. As I expectantly await Your return, I ask that You continue to pour out Your grace in my life so that I can be a blessing to my family, my church, and to the world around me. I give You thanks. Amen.

Day 3

Righteous by Faith

Searching the Scripture

Read Romans 4:16-22

> Therefore it is of faith that it might be according to grace, so that the promise might be sure to all the seed, not only to those who are of the law, but also to those who are of the faith of Abraham ... who, contrary to hope, in hope believed, so that he became the father of many nations, according to what was spoken, "So shall your descendants be." And not being weak in faith, he did not consider his own body, already dead (since he was about a hundred years old), and the deadness of Sarah's womb. He did not waver at the promise of God through unbelief, but was strengthened in faith, giving glory to God, and being fully convinced that what He had promised He was also able to perform. And therefore "it was accounted to him for righteousness."

Answer the Following Questions:

1. Explain how Paul connects "faith" and "grace" in this passage.

2. What was God's promise to Abraham (see Genesis 12)?

3. In what way were Abraham and Sarah "dead"?

4. Comment on Paul's phrase (taken from Genesis 15:6) that Abraham's faith was "accounted to him for righteousness."

Yielding to the Spirit

—Know—

All this week, we are studying the belief that "justification, regeneration, and the new birth are wrought by faith in the blood of Jesus." Today's lesson focuses especially on the phrase "wrought by faith." The word "wrought" is not used very much today unless you are building something out of wrought iron. It means "worked out, accomplished, achieved, or produced." Therefore, our statement of faith declares that all of the benefits and aspects of our salvation are accomplished by means of faith in God.

Saving faith includes our belief in the truth of the gospel (the birth, death, and resurrection of Jesus), and it also includes the act of trusting God for our salvation. We have confidence in the mercy of God through Jesus Christ.

The emphasis on salvation by faith was renewed during the Protestant Reformation (led by Martin Luther and John Calvin). However, it is not a new concept. In fact, the apostle Paul takes us all the way back to the Old Testament character of Abraham to show that faith has always been what God is looking for and what is necessary for us to have a relationship with God. Paul states, "For what does the Scripture say? 'Abraham believed

God, and it was accounted to him for righteousness'" (Romans 4:3).

In New Testament times, the Jewish people were concerned with all the details of the old covenant laws. They hoped to earn their righteousness by strictly obeying all God's commandments. The point that Jesus makes (and then Paul makes) is that everyone is guilty of disobedience, and everyone stands condemned of sin. Therefore, righteousness cannot be earned by our works. God wants our faith to be in Him alone. God wants our loyalty to Him and our trust in Him. If we give Him our faith, He will give us righteousness. Paul writes the following:

> Where is boasting then? It is excluded. By what law? Of works? No, but by the law of faith. Therefore we conclude that a man is justified by faith apart from the deeds of the law (Rom. 3:27-28).

—Be—

Jesus told the story of two men who went to the temple and prayed. God's response to their prayers sheds light on our discussion of justification by faith:

> Two men went up to the temple to pray, one a Pharisee and the other a tax collector. The Pharisee stood and prayed thus with himself, "God, I thank You that I am not like other men—extortioners, unjust, adulterers, or even as this tax collector. I fast twice a week; I give tithes of all that I possess." And the tax collector, standing afar off, would not so much as raise his eyes to heaven, but

> beat his breast, saying, "God, be merciful to me a sinner!" I tell you, this man went down to his house **justified** rather than the other (Luke 18:10-14).

Which one of these men reminds us of ourselves? Are we like the Pharisee, proud of our accomplishments and our religious devotion? Or, are we like the tax collector, trusting fully in God's mercy, humble, and repentant?

—Do—

In support of his commitment to the idea of justification by faith alone, the apostle Paul makes a list of his religious accomplishments; and then he declares them all to be "rubbish" when compared to the righteousness of God. He writes,

> If anyone else thinks he may have confidence in the flesh, I more so: circumcised the eighth day, of the stock of Israel, of the tribe of Benjamin, a Hebrew of the Hebrews; concerning the law, a Pharisee; concerning zeal, persecuting the church; concerning the righteousness which is in the law, blameless. But what things were gain to me, these I have counted loss for Christ. Yet indeed I also count all things loss for the excellence of the knowledge of Christ Jesus my Lord, for whom I have suffered the loss of all things, and count them as rubbish, that I may gain Christ and be found in Him, not having my own righteousness, which is from the law, but that which is through faith in Christ, the righteousness which is from God by faith (Philippians 3:4-9).

After you meditate for a few minutes on Paul's list of religious works, make a list of your own good works. Then, write the word "rubbish" over each one, and confess that it is your faith in Jesus Christ that makes you right with God.

Offer a Prayer

Lord God, I desire to be faithful and obedient to all Your commandments. I desire to love You and to love my neighbor, just as You have commanded. However, I realize that this obedience does not **make** me righteous. It is instead a thankful response to the righteousness that You have given to me by grace through faith. My righteousness comes from the merit of Jesus Christ, not from my own works. I give You thanks that I can rest in Christ's grace. In Jesus' name. Amen.

Day 4

Eternal Life

Searching the Scripture

Read Romans 6:23

> For the wages of sin is death, but the gift of God is **eternal life** in Christ Jesus our Lord.

Read 1 John 5:11-13

> And this is the testimony: that God has given us **eternal life**, and this life is in His Son. He who has the Son has life; he who does not have the Son of God does not have life. These things I have written to you who believe in the name of the Son of God, that you may know that you have **eternal life**, and that you may continue to believe in the name of the Son of God.

Answer the Following Questions:

1. Why do you think Paul uses the word "wages" when he refers to death, but he uses "gift" when he refers to eternal life?

2. Where is eternal life to be found?

3. Is the possession of eternal life something that we can "know"?

4. If we have eternal life, what should we "continue" to do?

Yielding to the Spirit

—Know—

Adam and Eve were created in the image of God, and they enjoyed unhindered access to God. They were fully alive spiritually. However, when they sinned, they came under the sentence of death. Spiritual death was immediate, and they lost the ability to fellowship with God. We inherited Adam's spiritual death.

Without Jesus Christ, we were spiritually dead in our trespasses and sins (Ephesians 2:5; Colossians 2:13). However, when we believed on Jesus and repented of our sins, the Holy Spirit made us spiritually alive. As we learned earlier, God's action of giving us new life is called "regeneration." We can say that our spiritual life is centered in Jesus because Jesus is life. Just before He raised Lazarus from the dead, Jesus said to Martha, "I am the resurrection and the life. He who believes in Me, though he may die, he shall live. And whoever lives and believes in Me shall never die" (John 11:25-26).

When the Bible speaks of the gift of eternal life, it refers both to the duration of life and to the quality of life. Regarding the duration of life, the "everlasting life" that Jesus gives (John 3:16) is life that will continue throughout eternity. Although our bodies may die, we will continue to live as spirits until the Resurrection, when our bodies will be raised up and given a new form called a "spiritual body" (1 Corinthians 15:44).

Regarding the quality of life, the New Testament emphasizes that we are living "between the times," that is, between what is called the "present age" and what is called the "coming age." The coming age is the time when Jesus will return to earth and establish His kingdom fully and completely. In the coming age, Jesus the Messiah will rule over the earth, and humanity will have unhindered access to the presence of God, just as Adam and Eve experienced in the Garden of Eden. Although we live in the "present age," Jesus has given us His Holy Spirit and made us spiritually alive. Therefore, the "coming age" has in some ways intruded into the present. The healings and miracles of Jesus were signs of the age to come. The love of God in our hearts is also a sign of the world to come. In summary, the life of the age to come is already partially available in Christ to the believer.

—Be—

On His way from Jerusalem to Galilee, Jesus stopped by Jacob's well in the region of Samaria. A Samaritan woman came to the well, and Jesus asked her for a drink. She was surprised that Jesus (who was Jewish) would even speak to a Samaritan because the Jews and Samaritans were enemies. The story continues:

> Jesus answered and said to her, "If you knew the gift of God, and who it is who says to you, 'Give Me a drink,' you would have asked Him, and He would have given you living water." The woman said to Him, "Sir, You have nothing to draw with, and the well is deep. Where then do You get that living water?" ... Jesus answered and said to her, "Whoever drinks of this water will thirst again, but whoever drinks of the water that I shall give him will never thirst. But the water that I shall give him will become in him a fountain of water springing up into everlasting life" (John 4:10-14).

The Samaritan woman believed on Jesus that day, and she brought many others to Jesus as well (John 4:39-41). The live of this woman and the lives of her family and friends were transformed by their encounter with Jesus.

—Do—

Have you encountered Jesus like the Samaritan woman? She received the word of Jesus as "living water," and it sprang up in her as a "fountain" of eternal life. Has Jesus transformed your life in a similar fashion? Our fellowship with God is ongoing. Make it a point to encounter Jesus every day through prayer, worship, and Bible study. Like the Samaritan woman, share the good news of Jesus with other people.

Offer a Prayer

Heavenly Father, I thank You that just like You gave eternal life to the Samaritan, You have given life to me. I was not searching for You, but You came searching for me. I praise You for Your grace and mercy. I appreciate the fountain of living water that is springing up in my heart and producing everlasting life. Please help me to take full advantage of the opportunities that You have placed before me to enjoy fellowship with You and to drink daily of the living water that You offer. I want all that You have for me, so I don't want to hold anything back from You. I thank You for Your great love for me. In Jesus' name. Amen.

Day 5

Living by Faith

Searching the Scripture

Read Hebrews 10:38 and 11:6-8

> Now the just shall live by faith; but if anyone draws back, My soul has no pleasure in him.
>
> But without faith it is impossible to please Him, for he who comes to God must believe that He is, and that He is a rewarder of those who diligently seek Him. By faith Noah, being divinely warned of things not yet seen, moved with godly fear, prepared an ark for the saving of his household, by which he condemned the world and became heir of the righteousness which is according to faith. By faith Abraham obeyed when he was called to go out to the place which he would receive as an inheritance. And he went out, not knowing where he was going.

Answer the Following Questions:

1. How would you describe the contrast between living by faith and drawing back?

2. What is necessary for pleasing God?

3. Noah had faith in God. What did his faith cause him to do?

4. Abraham had faith in God also. What is the connection between faith and obedience?

Yielding to the Spirit

—Know—

Abraham is called the "Father of the Faithful," and we are heirs of the faith of this great man of God. As Abraham's faith was tested over and over, he learned to live by faith, to trust God, to pray, and to persevere in the face of obstacles. The apostle Paul praises Abraham's faith, saying that he "believed God, and it was counted unto him as righteousness" (Romans 4:3 KJV). If we have faith in Christ, we are the children of Abraham (Galatians 3:7). Thus, Abraham is our example in faith. Just like Abraham, we are justified by faith.

In his first encounter with God, Abraham was required to walk by faith. God asked Abraham to leave all the securities of life for a land to which he had never been. By faith he obeyed God, not knowing where he went, but believing the promise of God. We like to hold on to those things that give us security, but God is trying to teach us that our security is in Him. "We walk by faith, not by sight" (2 Corinthians 5:7).

Then, when Abraham reached the Promised Land, his faith was tested by two obstacles: (1) Enemies filled the land. (2) Hardships fell into his pathway. The test of Abraham's faith is also the test of our faith today. Our profession of faith will be tested. Even when we are in the center of God's will, we will face trials and difficulties.

The apostle James tells us, "Be joyful when you fall into diverse temptations, knowing this, that the trying of your faith produces patience" (See James 1:2-3).

—Be—

Abraham and others after him have taught us to trust God, even when circumstances seem impossible. They have given us a heritage of faith—a faith that sees the invisible, a faith that accomplishes the impossible, a faith that obeys the incomprehensible, and a faith that endures the unbearable. Like our elders, we must be strong in faith.

The testing of faith is a major theme of the Book of Hebrews. The writer of Hebrews expressed a great truth when he said, "Without faith it is impossible to please God" (Hebrews 11:6). Faith is the key that unlocks the glories of heaven. God wants us to believe Him; but we often forget to believe, and we find ourselves seeking for visible evidence. Faith is not a vague belief or a kind of self-confidence. Faith is complete trust in God—trust in His love, trust in His power, and trust in His promise to be with us even to the end of the world (Matthew 28:20).

—Do—

Has God led you into some difficult situations? Are obstacles in your path? Do you find it hard to love some people? Do you recognize weaknesses in your own life?

Then pray and believe that God will help you. If you can believe, all things are possible (Mark 9:23). You only need a tiny bit of faith—faith the size of a mustard seed. For if you have faith the size of a mustard seed, you can say to the mountain, "Be removed and be cast into the sea," and it will be done. And NOTHING will be impossible to you! (See Matthew 17:20).

If you can believe, you will see the glory of God.

Pray a Prayer in Your Own Words

You may wish to write your prayer in the space below.

Group Discussion

Key Scripture—Exodus 15:1-18
(The Song of Moses)

> Then Moses and the children of Israel sang this song to the LORD, and spoke, saying: "I will sing to the LORD, for He has triumphed gloriously! The horse and its rider He has thrown into the sea! The LORD is my strength and song, and He has become my **salvation**; He is my God, and I will praise Him; my father's God, and I will exalt Him ... You in Your mercy have led forth the people whom You have redeemed; You have guided them in Your strength to Your holy habitation ... "The LORD shall reign forever and ever" (Exodus 15:1-18).

Opening—This is a time of fellowship and sharing about one another's lives.

Prayer—Ask the Lord to make His presence known and to begin the process of transformation into Christ-likeness for each participant.

Testimony—Have two or three group members give a testimony of how God is at work in their lives, whether it is through their daily encounters in this study, or some other way.

Discussion Questions:

1. Why did Moses and the people of Israel sing this song?

2. In the Book of Revelation, we hear about the people of God who are in heaven: "They sing the song of Moses, the servant of God, and the song of the Lamb, saying: Great and marvelous are Your works, Lord God Almighty! Just and true are Your ways, O King of the saints!" (Revelation 15:3) How is the song of Moses (Exodus 15) similar to the song of the Lamb (Revelation 7:9-12)?

3. The Bible often uses the word "salvation" to describe all that God has done for us. Let each person in the group explain what it means for God to be our "salvation."

4. In the Books of Exodus and Revelation, God's people sing. Discuss the role of singing and worship in the Christian life.

5. The Song of Moses includes the statement that "The Lord shall reign forever and ever." Discuss how our expectation for the coming kingdom of God can impact our lives of faith. How does our belief in the return of Jesus impact our lives?

Yielding to the Spirit

You can break up into small groups, or if your group is already small, remain together to finish the discussion. Take a moment to remind everyone of the Group Covenant, particularly the statement of confidentiality. Discuss any personal takeaways that you would like others to pray about with you. Conclude this conversation by praying for one another. Be attentive to the leading of the Holy Spirit in the use of spiritual gifts. If you feel led to share a word from the Lord, ask the group leader to come and witness what is being said, so as to provide a reliable witness for all involved.

This is the final lesson in this book; therefore, you should take a moment to bring closure to the last four weeks of study. Everyone is invited to continue the journey by digging in to the next book, titled, *A Sanctified People*, which will teach you in clear, everyday language the meaning of sanctification and holiness.

CHURCH OF GOD DECLARATION OF FAITH

We Believe:

1. In the verbal inspiration of the Bible.
2. In one God eternally existing in three persons; namely, the Father, Son, and Holy Ghost.
3. That Jesus Christ is the only begotten Son of the Father, conceived of the Holy Ghost, and born of the Virgin Mary. That Jesus was crucified, buried, and raised from the dead. That He ascended to heaven and is today at the right hand of the Father as the Intercessor.
4. That all have sinned and come short of the glory of God and that repentance is commanded of God for all and necessary for forgiveness of sins.
5. That justification, regeneration, and the new birth are wrought by faith in the blood of Jesus Christ.
6. In sanctification subsequent to the new birth, through faith in the blood of Christ; through the Word, and by the Holy Ghost.

7. Holiness to be God's standard of living for His people.
8. In the baptism with the Holy Ghost subsequent to a clean heart.
9. In speaking with other tongues as the Spirit gives utterance and that it is the initial evidence of the baptism of the Holy Ghost.
10. In water baptism by immersion, and all who repent should be baptized in the name of the Father, and of the Son, and of the Holy Ghost.
11. Divine healing is provided for all in the atonement.
12. In the Lord's Supper and washing of the saints' feet.
13. In the premillennial second coming of Jesus. First, to resurrect the righteous dead and to catch away the living saints to Him in the air. Second, to reign on the earth a thousand years.
14. In the bodily resurrection; eternal life for the righteous, and eternal punishment for the wicked.

FOR FURTHER READING

Arrington, French L., *Christian Doctrine: A Pentecostal Perspective* (3 vols.; Cleveland, TN: Pathway, 1992).

Arrington, French L., *Exploring the Declaration of Faith* (Cleveland, TN: Pathway Press, 2003).

Collins, Kenneth J., *The Scripture Way of Salvation: The Heart of John Wesley's Theology* (Nashville, TN: Abingdon Press, 1997).

Gause, R.H., *Living in the Spirit: The Way of Salvation* (Cleveland, TN: CPT Press, Rev. and expanded edn, 2009).